Martin Luther

Selections from the

World's Devotional Classics

Volume I V

Theologica Germanica to Leighton

Selections
from the
World's Devotional Classics

EDITED BY

Robert Scott and George W. Gilmore

Editors of The Homiletic Review

IN TEN VOLUMES

Volume I V

Theologica Germanica to Leighton

FUNK & WAGNALLS COMPANY

NEW YORK AND LONDON

Contents Volume Four

Selections

Prayers

vii

Contents

SELECTIONS FROM

Theologia Germanica

FROM THE TRANSLATION
BY
SUSANNA WINKWORTH

THEOLOGIA GERMANICA

A work belonging to the end of the fourteenth century and purporting to be a guide to the perfect life, which, in a mystical way, is to be found in union with God. It attained its fame chiefly because it was discovered and first published by Luther. First he came into possession of a small fragment which he published under the title, "Ein geystlich edles Buchleyn" (1516). Afterward he obtained a complete manuscript which he issued under the title, "Eyn deutsch Theologia" (Wittenberg, 1518), reprinted under the title, "Theologia Teütsch" (Augsburg, 1518). In the complete edition Luther appended a note to his preface according to which the author of the work was "a priest and custodian in the house of the Teutonic Masters at Frankfort." The same note is found also in the manuscript published by F. Pfeiffer "Theologia deutsch," Stuttgart, 1851 (English translation, "Theologia Germanica," London, 1854, 1874, and 1893), and hence is proved authentic. From a passage announcing his purpose it is evident that the author belonged to the so-called Friends of God, and that he wrote at a time when this community had to clear itself from the charge of connection with the sect of the "false free spirits" who tried to protect themselves with the name of the Friends of God, i.e., toward the end of the fourteenth century.

Of That Which Is Perfect and That Which Is In Part, and How That Which Is In Part Is Done Away, When That Which Is Perfect Is Come

St. Paul saith, "When that which is perfect is come, then that which is in part shall be done away" (Cor. 13:10). Now mark what is "that which is perfect" and "that which is in part."

"That which is perfect" is a Being, who hath comprehended and included all things in himself and his own substance, and without whom, and beside whom, there is no true substance, and in whom all things have their substance. For he is the substance of all things, and is in himself unchangeable and immovable, and changeth and moveth all things else. But "that which is in part," or the imperfect, is that which hath its source in, or springeth from the Perfect; just as a brightness or a visible appearance floweth out from the sun or a candle, and appeareth to be somewhat this or that. And it is called a creature; and of all these "things which are in part," none is the Perfect. So also the

Perfect is none of the things which are in part. The things which are in part can be apprehended, known, and exprest; but the Perfect can not be apprehended, known, or exprest by any creature as creature. Therefore we do not give a name to the Perfect, for it is none of these. The creature as creature can not know nor apprehend it, name nor conceive it. "Now when that which is perfect is come, then that which is in part shall be done away." But when doth it come? I say, when as much as may be, it is known, felt and tasted of the soul. For the lack lieth altogether in us, and not in it. In like manner the sun lighteth the whole world and is as near to one as another, yet a blind man seeth it not; but the fault thereof lieth in the blind man, not in the sun. And like as the sun may not hide its brightness, but must give light unto the earth (for heaven indeed draweth its light and heat from another fountain), so also God, who is the highest Good, willeth not to hide himself from any, wheresoever he findeth a devout soul, that is thoroughly purified from all creatures. For in what measure we put off the creature, in the same measure are we able to put on the Creator; neither more nor less. For if mine eye is to see anything, it must be single, or else be purified from all other things; and where heat and light enter in, cold and darkness must needs depart; it can not be otherwise.

But one might say, "Now since the Perfect can not be known nor apprehended of any creature but the soul is a creature, how can it be known by the soul?" Answer: This is why we say, "by the soul as a creature." We mean it is impossible to the creature in virtue of its creature-nature and qualities, that by which it saith "I" and "myself." For in whatsoever creature the Perfect shall be known, therein creature-nature, qualities, the I, the self and the like, must all be lost and done away. This is the meaning of that saying of St. Paul: "When that which is perfect is come" (that is, when it is known), "then that which is in part" (to wit, creature-nature, qualities, the I, the self, the mine) will be despised and counted for naught. So long as we think much of these things, cleave to them with love, joy, pleasure or desire, so long remaineth the Perfect unknown to us.

But it might further be said, "thou sayest, beside the Perfect there is no substance, yet sayest again that somewhat floweth out from it: now is not that which hath flowed out from it, something beside it?" Answer: This is why we say, beside it, or without it, there is no true substance. That which hath flowed forth from it is no true substance, and hath no substance except in the Perfect, but is an accident, or a brightness, or a visible appearance, which is no substance, and hath no substance except in the fire whence the brightness flowed forth, such as the sun or a candle.

II

Of What Sin Is, and How We Must Not Take Unto Ourselves Any Good Thing, Seeing That It Belongeth Unto the True Good Alone

The Scripture and the faith and the truth say, sin is naught else, but that the creature turneth away from the unchangeable Good and betaketh itself to the changeable; that is to say, that it turneth away from the perfect, to "that which is in part" and imperfect, and most often to itself. Now mark: when the creature claimeth for its own anything good, such as substance, life, knowledge, power, and in short whatever we should call good, as if it were that, or possest that, or that were itself, or that proceeded from it—as often as this cometh to pass, the creature goeth astray. What did the devil do else, or what was his going astray and his fall else, but that he claimed for himself to be also somewhat, and would have it that somewhat was his, and somewhat was due to him? This setting up of a claim and his I and me and mine, these were his going astray, and his fall. And thus it is to this day.

III

How Man's Fall and Going Astray Must Be Amended as Adam's Fall Was

What else did Adam do but this same thing? It is said, it was because Adam ate the apple that he was lost, or fell. I say, it was because of his claiming something for his own, and because of his I, mine, me, and the like. Had he eaten seven apples, and yet never claimed anything for his own, he would not have fallen: but as soon as he called something his own, he fell, and would have fallen if he had never touched an apple. Behold! I have fallen a hundred times more often and deeply, and gone a hundred times farther astray than Adam; and not all mankind could amend his fall, or bring him back from going astray. But how shall my fall be amended? It must be healed as Adam's fall was healed, and on the self-same wise. By whom, and on what wise was that healing brought to pass? Mark this: man could not without God, and God should not without man. Wherefore God took human

7

nature or manhood upon himself and was made man, and man was made divine. Thus the healing was brought to pass. So also must my fall be healed. I can not do the work without God, and God may not or will not without me; for if it shall be accomplished, in me, too, God must be made man; in such sort that God must take to himself all that is in me, within and without, so that there may be nothing in me which striveth against God or hindereth his work. Now if God took to himself all men that are in the world, or ever were, and were made man in them, and they were made divine in him, and this work were not fulfilled in me, my fall and my wandering would never be amended except it were fulfilled in me also. And in this bringing back and healing, I can, or may, or shall do nothing of myself, but just simply yield to God, so that he alone may do all things in me and work, and I may suffer him and all his work and his divine will. And because I will not do so, but I count myself to be my own, and say, "I," "mine," "me" and the like, God is hindered, so that he can not do his work in me alone and without hindrance; for this cause my fall and my going astray remain unhealed. Behold! this all cometh of my claiming somewhat for my own.

[Chap. IV. shows: How man, when he claimeth any good thing for his own, falleth and toucheth <u>G</u>od in his honor.]

V

How We Are to Take That Saying, That We Must Come to Be Without Will, Wisdom, Love, Desire, Knowledge and the Like

Certain men say that we ought to be without will, wisdom, love, desire, knowledge and the like. Hereby is not to be understood that there is to be no knowledge in man, and that God is not to be loved by him, nor desired and longed for, nor praised and honored; for that were a great loss, and man were like the beasts and as the brutes that have no reason. But it meaneth that man's knowledge should be so clear and perfect that he should acknowledge of a truth that in himself he neither hath nor can do any good thing, and that none of his knowledge, wisdom and art, his will, love and good works do come from himself, nor are of man, nor of any creature, but that all these are of the eternal God, from whom they all proceed. As Christ himself saith, "Without me, ye can do nothing" (John 15:5). St. Paul saith also, "What hast thou that thou hast not received?" (1 Cor. 4:7). As much as to say—nothing. "Now, if thou didst receive it, why dost thou glory as if thou hadst not received it?" Again he saith, "Not that

we are sufficient of ourselves to think anything
as of ourselves, but our sufficiency is of God"
(2 Cor. 3:5). Now, when a man duly perceiveth these things in himself, he and the
creature fall behind, and he doth not call
anything his own, and the less he taketh this
knowledge unto himself, the more perfect doth
it become. So also is it with the will, and love,
and desire, and the like. For the less we call
these things our own, the more perfect, and
noble, and godlike do they become, and the
more we think them our own, the baser and
less pure and perfect do they become.

Behold on this sort must we cast all things
from us, and strip ourselves of them; we must
refrain from claiming anything for our own.
When we do this, we shall have the best,
fullest, clearest and noblest knowledge that a
man can have, and also the noblest and purest
love, will and desire; for then these will be all
of God alone. It is much better that they
should be God's than the creature's. Now
that I ascribe anything good to myself, as if
I were, or had done, or knew, or could perform any good thing, or that it were mine,
this is all of sin and folly. For if the truth
were rightly known by me, I should also know
that I am not that good thing, and that it is
not mine nor of me, and that I do not know
it, and can not do it, and the like. If this came

to pass, I should needs cease to call anything my own.

It is better that God, or his works, should be known, as far as it be possible to us, and loved, praised and honored, and the like, and even that man should but vainly imagine he loveth or praiseth God, than that God should be altogether unpraised, unloved, unhonored and unknown. For when the vain imagination and ignorance are turned into an understanding and knowledge of the truth, the claiming anything for our own will cease of itself. Then the man says: "Behold! I, poor fool that I was, imagined it was I; but, behold! it is, and was, of a truth, God!"

VI

How That Which Is Best and Noblest Should Also Be Loved Above All Things by Us, Merely Because It Is the Best

A master called Boetius saith, "It is of sin that we do not love that which is best." He hath spoken the truth. That which is best should be the dearest of all things to us; and in our love of it, neither helpfulness nor unhelpfulness, advantage nor injury, gain nor

Devotional Classics

loss, honor nor dishonor, praise nor blame, nor anything of the kind should be regarded; but what is in truth the noblest and best of all things, should be also the dearest of all things, and that for no other cause than that it is the noblest and best.

Hereby may a man order his life within and without. His outward life: for among the creatures one is better than another, according as the Eternal Good manifesteth itself and worketh more in one than in another. Now that creature in which the Eternal Good most manifesteth itself, shineth forth, worketh, is most known and loved, is the best, and that wherein the Eternal Good is least manifested is the least Good of all creatures. Therefore when we have to do with the creatures, and hold converse with them, and take note of their diverse qualities, the best creatures must always be the dearest to us, and we must cleave to them, and unite ourselves to them, above all to those which we attribute to God as belonging to him or divine, such as wisdom, truth, kindness, peace, love, justice, and the like. Hereby shall we order our outward man, and all that is contrary to these virtues we must eschew and flee from.

But if our inward man were to make a leap and spring into the Perfect, we should find and taste how that the Perfect is without

12

measure, number or end, better and nobler
than all which is imperfect and in part, and
the Eternal above the temporal or perishable,
and the fountain and source above all that
floweth or can ever flow from it. Thus that
which is imperfect and in part would become
tasteless and be as nothing to us. Be assured
of this: All that we have said must come to
pass if we are to love that which is noblest,
highest and best.

[Chap. VII. treats of the Eyes of the Spirit wherewith
Man looketh into Eternity and into Time, and how the
one is hindered of the other in its working.]

VIII

How the Soul of Man, While It Is Yet In the Body, May Obtain a Foretaste of Eternal Blessedness

It hath been asked whether it be possible for
the soul, while it is yet in the body, to reach
so high as to cast a glance into eternity, and
receive a foretaste of eternal life and eternal
blessedness. This is commonly denied; and
truly so in a sense. For it indeed can not
be so long as the soul is taking heed to the
body, and the things which minister and appertain thereto, and to time and the creature,
and is disturbed and troubled and distracted

13

thereby. For if the soul shall rise to such a state, she must be quite pure, wholly stript and bare of all images, and be entirely separate from all creatures, and above all, from herself. Now, many think this is not to be done, and is impossible in this present time. But St. Dionysius maintains that it is possible, as we find from his words in his epistle to Timothy, where he saith: "For the beholding of the hidden things of God, shalt thou forsake sense and the things of the flesh, and all that the senses can apprehend, and that reason of her own powers can bring forth, and all things created and uncreated that reason is able to comprehend and know, and shall take thy stand upon an utter abandonment of thyself, and as knowing none of the aforesaid things, and enter into union with him who is, and who is above all existence and all knowledge." Now if he did not hold this to be possible in this present time, why should he teach it and enjoin it on us in this present time? But it behoveth you to know that a master hath said on this passage of St. Dionysius, that it is possible, and may happen to a man often, till he becomes so accustomed to it as to be able to look into eternity whenever he will. For when a thing is at first very hard to a man and strange, and seemingly quite impossible, if he put all his strength and energy into it, and persevere therein, that will afterward grow quite light and easy which he at first thought quite out of reach, seeing that it is of no use to begin any work unless it may be brought to a good end.

And a single one of these excellent glances is better, worthier, higher and more pleasing to God than all that the creature can perform as a creature. And as soon as a man turneth himself in spirit, and with his whole heart and mind entereth into the mind of God which is above time, all that ever he hath lost is restored in a moment. And if a man were to do thus a thousand times in a day, each time a fresh and real union would take place; and in this sweet and divine work standeth the truest and fullest union that may be in this present time. For he who hath attained thereto, asketh nothing further, for he hath found the kingdom of heaven and eternal life on earth.

[Chaps. IX.–XI. have the following captions: IX. How it is more profitable for a Man that he should perceive to what end God will use him, than if he knew all that God had ever wrought, or would ever work. X. How the perfect Men have no other Desire than that they may be used of God. XI. How a righteous Man in this present Time is brought into Hell, and there can not be comforted, and how he is taken out of Hell and carried into Heaven, and there can not be troubled.]

XII

Touching That True Inward Peace, Which Christ Left to His Disciples

Many say they have no peace nor rest, but
so many crosses and trials, afflictions and sorrows, that they know not how they shall ever
get through them. Now he who in truth will
perceive and take note, perceiveth clearly that
true peace and rest lie not in outward things;
for if it were so, the Evil Spirit also would
have peace when things go according to his
will, which is nowise the case; for the prophet
declareth, "There is no peace, saith my God,
to the wicked" (Isa. 57:21). And therefore
we must consider and see what is that peace
which Christ left to his disciples at the last,
when he said: "My peace I leave with you,
my peace I give unto you" (John 14:27).
We may perceive that in these words Christ
did not mean a bodily and outward peace;
for his beloved disciples, with all his friends
and followers, have ever suffered, from the beginning, great affliction, persecution, nay,
often martyrdom, as Christ himself said: "In
this world ye shall have tribulation" (John
16:33). But Christ meant that true, inward
peace of the heart, which beginneth here and
endureth forever hereafter. Therefore he
said: "Not as the world giveth," for the

world is false and deceiveth in her gifts; she promiseth much and performeth little. Moreover, there liveth no man on earth who may always have rest and peace, without troubles and crosses, with whom things always go according to his will; there is always something to be suffered here, turn which way thou wilt. And as soon as thou art quit of one assault, perhaps two come in its place. Wherefore yield thyself willingly to them, and seek only that true peace of the heart which none can take away from thee, that thou mayest overcome all assaults.

Thus, then, Christ meant that inward peace which can break through all assaults and crosses of oppression, suffering, misery, humiliation and what more there may be of the like, so that a man may be joyful and patient therein, like the beloved disciples and followers of Christ. Now he who will in love give his whole diligence and might thereto, will verily come to know that true eternal peace which is God himself, as far as it is possible to a creature; insomuch that what was bitter to him before shall become sweet, and his heart shall remain unmoved under all changes, at all times, and after this life he shall attain unto everlasting peace.

[Chap. XIII. shows how a man may cast aside Types and Symbols too soon.]

XIV

Of Three Stages by Which a Man Is Led Upward Till He Attaineth True Perfection

Now be assured that no one can be enlightened unless he be first cleansed or purified and stript. So also, no one can be united with God unless he be first enlightened. Thus there are three stages: first, the purification; secondly, the enlightening; thirdly, the union. The purification concerneth those who are beginning or repenting, and is brought to pass in a threefold wise; by contrition and sorrow for sin, by full confession, by hearty amendment. The enlightening belongeth to such as are growing, and also taketh place in three ways: to wit, by the eschewal of sin, by the practise of virtue and good works, and by the willing endurance of all manner of temptation and trials. The union belongeth to such as are perfect, and also is brought to pass in three ways: to wit, by pureness and singleness of heart, by love, and by the contemplation of God, the Creator of all things.

XV.

How All Men Are Dead In Adam and Are Made Alive Again In Christ, and of True Obedience and Disobedience

All that in Adam fell and died, was raised again and made alive in Christ, and all that rose up and was made alive in Adam, fell and died in Christ. But what was that? I answer, true obedience and disobedience. But what is true obedience? I answer, that a man should so stand free, being quit of himself, that is, of his I, and me, and self, and mine, and the like, that in all things, he should no more seek or regard himself, than if he did not exist, and should take as little account of himself as if he were not, and another had done all his works. Likewise he should count all the creatures for nothing. What is there then, which is, and which we may count for somewhat? I answer, nothing but that which we may call God. Behold! this is very obedience in the truth, and thus it will be in a blessed eternity. There nothing is sought nor thought of, nor loved, but the one thing only.

Hereby we may mark what disobedience is: to wit, that a man maketh some account of himself, and thinketh that he is, and knoweth, and can do somewhat, and seeketh himself and his own ends in the things around him, and hath regard to and loveth himself, and the like. Man is created for true obedience, and is bound of right to render it to God. And this obedience fell and died in Adam, and rose again and lived in Christ. Yea, Christ's human nature was so utterly bereft of self, and apart from all creatures, as no man's ever was, and was nothing else but "a house and habitation of God." Neither of that in him which belonged to God, nor of that which was a living human nature and a habitation of God, did he, as man, claim anything for his own. His human nature did not even take unto himself the Godhead, whose dwelling it was, nor anything that this same Godhead willed, or did or left undone in him, nor yet any thing of all that his human nature did or suffered; but in Christ's human nature there was no claiming of anything, nor seeking, nor desire, saving that what was due might be rendered to the Godhead, and he did not call this very desire his own. Of this matter no more can be said or written here; for it is unspeakable, and was never yet and never will be fully uttered; for it can neither be spoken nor written but by him who is and knows its ground; that is, God himself, who can do all things well.

[Chap. XVI. telleth us what is the old Man, and what is the new Man; and XVII., how we are not to take unto ourselves what we have done well.]

XVIII

How That the Life of Christ Is the Noblest and Best Life, and How a Careless Life of False Freedom Is the Worst Life

Of a truth we ought to know and believe that there is no life so noble and good and well pleasing to God, as the life of Christ, and yet it is to nature and selfishness the bitterest life. A life of carelessness and freedom is to nature and the self and the me the sweetest and pleasantest life, but is not the best; and in some men may become the worst. But tho Christ's life be the most bitter of all, yet it is to be preferred above all. Hereby shall ye mark this: There is an inward sight which hath power to perceive the one true Good, and that it is neither this nor that, but that of which St. Paul saith: "when that which is perfect is come, then that which is in part shall be done away" (1 Cor. 13:10). By this he meaneth that the Whole and Perfect excelleth all the fragments, and that all which is in part and imperfect, is as naught compared to the Perfect. Thus likewise all knowledge of the parts is swallowed up when the Whole is known; and where that Good is known, it can not but be longed for and loved so greatly, that all other love wherewith the man hath loved himself and other things, fadeth away. And that inward sight likewise perceiveth what is best and noblest in all things, and loveth it in the one true Good, and only for the sake of that true Good.

Behold! where there is this inward sight, the man perceiveth of a truth that Christ's life is the best and noblest life, and therefore the most to be preferred, and he willingly accepteth and endureth it, without a question or a complaint, whether it please or offend nature or other men, whether he like or dislike it, find it sweet or bitter, and the like. And therefore wherever this perfect and true Good is known, there also the life of Christ must be led, until the death of the body. And he who vainly thinketh otherwise is deceived, and he who saith otherwise, lieth, and in what man the life of Christ is not, of him the true Good and eternal Truth will never more be known.

[Chap. XIX. tells how we can not come to the true Light by Questioning or Reading, or by natural Skill and Reason, but by renouncing ourselves and all Things; and Chap. XX., how, seeing that the Life of Christ is most bitter to Nature and Self, Nature will have none of it, and chooseth a false, careless Life, as is most convenient to her.]

XXI

How a Friend of Christ Willingly Fulfilleth By His Outward Works, Such Things as Must Be and Ought to Be, and Doth Not Concern Himself With the Rest

Now, it may be asked, what is the state of a man who followeth the true Light to the utmost of his power? I answer truly, it will never be declared aright, for he who is not such a man, can neither understand nor know it, and he who is, knoweth it indeed; but he can not utter it, for it is unspeakable. Therefore let him who would know it, give his whole diligence that he may enter therein; then will he see and find what hath never been uttered by man's lips. However, I believe that such a man hath liberty as to his outward walk and conversation, so long as they consist with what must be or ought to be; but they may not consist with what he merely willeth to be. But oftentimes a man maketh to himself many must-be's and ought-to-be's which are false. The which ye may see hereby, that when a man is moved by his pride or covetousness or other evil dispositions to do or leave undone anything, he ofttimes saith, "It must needs be so, and ought to be so." Or if he is driven to, or held back from anything by the desire to find favor in men's eyes, or by love, friendship, enmity, or the lusts and appetites of his body, he saith, "It must needs be so, and ought to be so." Yet behold, that is utterly false. Had we no must-be's, nor ought-to-be's, but such as God and the truth show us, and constrain us to, we should have less, forsooth, to order and do than now; for we make to ourselves much disquietude and difficulty which we might well be spared and raised above.

[Chap. XXII. shows how the Spirit of God, and sometimes also the Evil Spirit may possess a Man and have the Mastery over him; Chap. XXIII., how he who will submit himself to God and be obedient must be ready to bear all Things; and Chap. XXIV., four things that are needful before a Man can receive Truth and be possest with the Spirit.]

XXV

Of Two Evil Fruits That Do Spring Up From the Seed of the Evil Spirit, and Are Two Sisters Who Love to Dwell Together, the One Is Called Spiritual Pride and High-mindedness, the Other Is False, Lawless Freedom

Now, after that a man hath walked in all the ways that lead him unto the truth, and exercised himself therein, not sparing his

labor; now, as often and as long as he dreameth that his work is altogether finished, and he
is by this time quite dead to the world, and
come out from self and given up to God alone,
behold! the devil cometh and soweth his seed
in the man's heart. From this seed spring
two fruits; the one is spiritual fulness or
pride, the other is false, lawless freedom.
These are two sisters who love to be together.
Now, it beginneth on this wise: the devil puff-
eth up the man, till he thinketh himself to
have climbed the topmost pinnacle, and to
have come so near to heaven that he no longer
needeth Scripture, nor teaching, nor this nor
that, but is altogether raised above any need.
Whereupon there ariseth a false peace and
satisfaction with himself, and then it followeth that he saith or thinketh: "Yea, now I am
above all other men, and know and understand
more than any one in the world; therefore it is
certainly just and reasonable that I should
be the lord and commander of all creatures,
and that all creatures, and especially all men,
should serve me and be subject unto me."
And then he seeketh and desireth the same,
and taketh it gladly from all creatures, especially men, and thinketh himself well
worthy of all this, and that it is his due, and
looketh on men as if they were the beasts of
the field, and thinketh himself worthy of all

that ministereth to his body and life and
nature, in profit, or joy, or pleasure, or even
pastime and amusement, and he seeketh and
taketh it wherever he findeth opportunity.
And whatever is done or can be done for him,
seemeth him all too little and too poor, for he
thinketh himself worthy of still more and
greater honor than can be rendered to him.
And of all the men who serve him and are
subject to him, even if they be downright
thieves and murderers, he saith nevertheless,
that they have faithful, noble hearts, and have
great love and faithfulness to the truth and
to poor men. And such men are praised by
him, and he seeketh them and followeth after
them wherever they be. But he who doth not
order himself according to the will of these
high-minded men, nor is subject unto them, is
not sought after by them, nay, more likely
blamed and spoken ill of, even tho he were
as holy as St. Peter himself. And seeing that
this proud and puffed-up spirit thinketh that
she needeth neither Scripture, nor instruc-
tion, nor anything of the kind, therefore she
giveth no heed to the admonitions, order,
laws and precepts of the holy Christian
Church, nor to the sacraments, but mocketh at
them and at all men who walk according to
these ordinances and hold them in reverence.

Hereby we may plainly see that those two sisters dwell together.

Moreover since this sheer pride thinketh to know and understand more than all men besides, therefore she chooseth to prate more than all other men, and would fain have her opinions and speeches to be alone regarded and listened to, and counteth all that others think and say to be wrong, and holdeth it in derision as a folly.

XXVI

Touching Poorness of Spirit and True Humility, and Whereby We May Discern the True and Lawful Free Men, Whom the Truth Hath Made Free

But it is quite otherwise where there is poorness of spirit, and true humility; and it is so because it is found and known of a truth that a man, of himself and his own power, is nothing, hath nothing, can do and is capable of nothing but only infirmity and evil. Hence followeth that the man findeth himself altogether unworthy of all that hath been or ever will be done for him, by God or the creatures, and that he is a debtor to God and also to all the creatures in God's stead, both to bear with, and to labor for, and to serve them. And

27

therefore he doth not in any wise stand up for his own rights, but from the humility of his heart he saith, "It is just and reasonable that God and all creatures should be against me, and have a right over me, and to me, and that I should not be against any one, nor have a right to any thing." Hence it followeth that the man doth not and will not crave or beg for any thing, either from God or the creatures, beyond mere needful things, and for those only with shamefacedness, as a favor and not as a right. And he will not minister unto or gratify his body or any of his natural desires beyond what is needful, nor allow that any should help or serve him except in case of necessity, and then always in trembling; for he hath no right to any thing, and therefore he thinketh himself unworthy of any thing. So likewise all his own discourse, ways, words and works seem to this man a thing of naught and a folly. Therefore he speaketh little, and doth not take upon himself to admonish or rebuke any, unless he be constrained thereto by love or faithfulness toward God, and even then he doth it in fear, and so little as may be.

Moreover, when a man hath this poor and humble spirit, he cometh to see and understand aright, how that all men are bent upon themselves, and inclined to evil and sin, and that on this account it is needful and profitable that there be order, customs, law and precepts, to the end that the blindness and foolishness of men may be corrected, and that vice and wickedness may be kept under, and constrained to seemliness. For without ordinances, men would be much more mischievous and ungovernable than dogs and cattle. And few have come to the knowledge of the truth, but what have begun with holy practises and ordinances, and exercised themselves therein so long as they knew nothing more nor better.

Therefore one who is poor in spirit and of a humble mind doth not despise or make light of law, order, precepts and holy customs, nor yet of those who observe and cleave wholly to them, but with loving pity and gentle sorrow, crieth: "Almighty Father, thou Eternal Truth, I make my lament unto thee, and it grieveth thy Spirit, too, that through man's blindness, infirmity, and sin, that is made needful and must be, which in deed and truth were neither needful nor right." For those who are perfect are under no law.

So order, laws, precepts and the like are merely an admonition to men who understand nothing better and know and perceive not wherefore all law and order is ordained. And the perfect accept the law along with such ignorant men as understand and know nothing better, and practise it with them, to the intent that they may be restrained thereby, and kept from evil ways, or if it be possible, brought to something higher.

Behold! all that we have said of poverty and humility is so of a truth, and we have the proof and witness thereof in the pure life of Christ, and in his words. For he both practised and fulfilled every work of true humility and all other virtues, as shineth forth in his holy life, and he saith also expressly: "Learn of me, for I am meek and lowly of heart, and ye shall find rest unto your souls" (Matt. 11: 29). Moreover, he did not despise and set at naught the law and the commandments, nor yet the men who are under the law. He saith: "I am not come to destroy the law or the prophets, but to fulfil." But he saith further, that to keep them is not enough, we must press forward to what is higher and better, as is indeed true. He saith: "Except your righteousness shall exceed the righteousness of the scribes and Pharisees, ye shall in no case enter into the kingdom of heaven" (Matt. 5: 20). For the law forbiddeth evil works, but Christ condemneth also evil thoughts; the law alloweth us to take vengeance on our enemies, but Christ commandeth us to love them. The law forbiddeth not the good things of this world, but he counselleth us to despise them.

And he hath set his seal upon all he said, with his own holy life; for he taught nothing that he did not fulfil in work, and he kept the law and was subject unto it to the end of his mortal life. Likewise St. Paul saith: "Christ was made under the law to redeem them that were under the law" (Gal. 4:4). That is, that he might bring them to something higher and nearer to himself. He said again, "The Son of man came not to be ministered unto but to minister" (Matt. 20:28).

In a word: in Christ's life and words and works we find nothing but true, pure humility and poverty such as we have set forth. And therefore where God dwelleth in a man, and the man is a true follower of Christ, it will be, and must be, and ought to be the same. But where there is pride, and a haughty spirit, and a light, careless mind, Christ is not, nor any true follower of his.

Christ said: "My soul is troubled, even unto death." He meaneth his bodily death. That is to say: from the time that he was born of Mary until his death on the cross he had not one joyful day, but only trouble, sorrow and contradiction. Therefore it is just and reasonable that his servants should be even as their Master. Christ saith also: "Blessed are the poor in spirit" (that is, those who are truly humble), "for theirs is the kingdom of heaven." And thus we find it of a truth, where God is made man. For in Christ and in all his true followers, there must needs be thorough humility and poorness of spirit, a lowly retiring disposition, and a heart laden with a secret sorrow and mourning, so long as this mortal life lasteth. And he who dreameth otherwise is deceived, and deceiveth others with him as aforesaid. Therefore nature and self always avoid this life, and cling to a life of false freedom and ease as we have said.

Behold! now cometh an Adam or an Evil Spirit, wishing to justify himself and make excuse, and saith: "Thou wilt almost have it that Christ was bereft of self and the like, yet he spake often of himself, and glorified himself in this and that." Answer: when a man in whom the truth worketh hath and ought to have a will toward any thing, his will and endeavor and works are for no end but that the truth may be seen and manifested; and this will was in Christ, and to this end, words and works are needful. And what Christ did because it was the most profitable and best means thereunto, he no more took unto himself than anything else that happened. Dost thou say now: "Then there was a Wherefore in Christ?" I answer, if thou wert to ask the sun, "why shinest thou?" he would say: "I must shine, and can not do otherwise, for it is my nature and property; but this my property, and the light I give, is not of myself, and I do not call it mine." So likewise is it with God and Christ and all who are godly and belong unto God. In them is no willing, nor working nor desiring but has for its end, goodness, as goodness, for the sake of goodness, and they have no other Wherefore than this.

XXVII

How We Are to Take Christ's Words When He Bade Us Forsake All Things; and Wherein the Union With the Divine Will Standeth

Now, according to what hath been said, ye must observe that when we say, as Christ also saith, that we ought to resign and forsake all things, this is not to be taken in the sense that a man is neither to do nor to purpose anything; for a man must always have something to do and to order so long as he liveth. But we are to understand by it that the union with God standeth not in any man's powers, in his working or abstaining, perceiving or knowing, nor in that of all the creatures taken together.

Now what is this union? It is that we should

be of a truth purely, simply, and wholly at one with the one eternal will of God, or altogether without will, so that the created will should flow out into the eternal will, and be swallowed up and lost therein, so that the eternal will alone should do and leave undone in us. Now mark what may help or further us toward this end. Behold, neither exercises, nor words, nor works, nor any creature nor creature's work, can do this. In this wise therefore must we renounce and forsake all things, that we must not imagine or suppose that any words, works, or exercises, any skill or cunning or any created thing, can help or serve us thereto. Therefore we must suffer these things to be what they are, and enter into the union with God. Yet outward things must be, and we must do and refrain so far as is necessary, especially we must sleep and wake, walk and stand still, speak and be silent, and much more of the like. These must go on so long as we live.

XXVIII

How, After a Union With the Divine Will, the Inward Man Standeth Immovable, the While the Outward Man Is Moved Hither and Thither

Now, when this union truly cometh to pass and becometh established, the inward man standeth henceforward immovable in this union; and God suffereth the outward man to be moved hither and thither, from this to that, of such things as are necessary and right. So that the outward man saith in sincerity, 'I have no will to be or not to be, to live or die, to know or not to know, to do or to leave undone and the like; but I am ready for all that is to be, or ought to be, and obedient thereunto, whether I have to do or to suffer.'' And thus the outward man hath no Wherefore or purpose, but only to do his part to further the eternal will. For it is perceived of a truth, that the inward man shall stand immovable, and that it is needful for the outward man to be moved. And if the inward man have any Wherefore in the actions of the outward man, he saith only that such things must be and ought to be, as are ordained by the eternal will. And where God himself dwelleth in the man, it is thus; as we plainly see in Christ. Moreover, where there is this union, which is the offspring of a divine light and dwelleth in its beams, there is no spiritual pride, or irreverent spirit, but boundless humility, and a lowly broken heart; also an honest blameless walk, justice, peace, content and all that is of virtue must needs be there. Where they are not, there is no right union, as we have said. For just as neither this thing nor that can bring about or further this union, so there is nothing which hath power to frustrate or hinder it, save the man himself with his self-will, that doeth him his great wrong.

[Chap. XXIX. teaches how a Man may not attain so high before Death as not to be moved or touched by outward things; Chap. XXX., how we may come to be beyond and above all Custom, Order, and the like; Chap. XXXI., how we are not to cast off the life of Christ, but practise and walk in it until death; and Chap. XXXII., how God is a true, simple, perfect Good, and how he is a Light and a Reason and all Virtues, and how what is highest and best, that is, God, ought to be most loved.]

XXXIII

How When a Man Is Made Truly Godlike, His Love Is Pure and Unmixed, and He Loveth All Creatures, and Doth His Best for Them

In a truly godlike man, his love is pure and unmixed, and full of kindness, insomuch that he can not but love in sincerity all men and things, and wish well, and do good to them, and rejoice in their welfare. Yea, let them do what they will to such a man, do him wrong or kindness, bear him love or hatred or the like, yea, if one could kill such a man a hundred times over, and he always came to life again, he could not but love the very man who had so often slain him, altho he had been treated so unjustly, and wickedly, and cruelly by him, and could not but wish well, and do well to him, and show him the very greatest kindness in his power, if the other would but receive and take it at his hands. The proof and witness whereof may be seen in Christ; for he said to Judas, when he betrayed him: "Friend, wherefore art thou come?" Just as if he had said: "Thou hatest me, and art mine enemy, yet I love thee, and am thy friend. Thou desirest and rejoicest in my affliction, and dost the worst thou canst unto me; yet I desire and wish thee all good, and would fain give it thee, and do it for thee, if thou wouldst but take and receive it." As tho God in human nature were saying: "I am pure, simple Goodness, and therefore I can not will, or desire, or rejoice in, or do, or give anything but goodness. If I am to reward thee for thy evil and wickedness, I must do it with goodness, for I am and have nothing else." Hence therefore God, in a man who is "made partaker of his nature," desireth and taketh no revenge for all the wrong that is or can be done unto him. This we see in Christ when he said: "Father, forgive them, for they know not what they do."

Likewise it is God's property that he doth not constrain any by force to do or not to do anything, but he alloweth every man to do and leave undone according to his will, whether it be good or bad, and resisteth none. This too we see in Christ, who would not resist or defend himself when his enemies laid hands on him. And when Peter would have defended him, he said unto Peter: "Put up thy sword into the sheath: the cup which my Father hath given me, shall I not drink it?" Neither may a man who is made a partaker of the divine nature, oppress or grieve any one. That is, it never entereth into his thoughts, or intents, or wishes to cause pain or distress to any, either by deed or neglect, by speech or silence.

XXXIV

How That If a Man Will Attain to That Which Is Best, He Must Forswear His Own Will; and He Who Helpeth a Man to His Own Will Helpeth Him to the Worst Thing He Can

Some may say: "Now since God willeth and desireth and doth the best that may be to every one, he ought so to help each man and order things for him, that they should fall out according to his will and fulfil his desires, so that one might be a pope, another a bishop, and so forth." Be assured, he who helpeth a man to his own will, helpeth him to the worst that he can. For the more a man followeth after his own self-will, and self-will groweth in him, the farther off is he from God, the true Good, for nothing burneth in hell but self-will. Therefore it hath been said, "Put off thine own will, and there will be no hell." Now God is very willing to help a man and bring him to that which is best in itself, and is of all things the best for man. But to this end, all self-will must depart, as we have said. And God would fain give man his help and counsel thereunto, for so long as a man is seeking his own good, he doth not seek what is best for him, and will never find it. For a man's highest good would be and truly is, that he should not seek himself nor his own things, nor be his own end in any respect, either in things spiritual or things natural, but should seek only the praise and glory of God and his holy will. This doth God teach and admonish us.

Let him therefore who wisheth that God should help him to what is best, and best for him, give diligent heed to God's counsels and teachings, and obey his commandments; thus, and not else, will he have, and hath already, God's help. Now God teacheth and admonisheth man to forsake himself and all things, and to follow him only. "For he who loveth his soul,"[1] that is himself, and will guard it and keep it, "he shall lose it"; that is, he who seeketh himself and his own advantage in all things, in so doing loseth his soul. "But he who hateth his soul for my sake shall keep it unto life eternal"; that is, he who forsaketh himself and his own things, and giveth up his

---

[1] Mark 8 : 35. Our authorized version uses the word "life," in this verse, but as that would not quite bring out the force of the original, I have ventured to use the same word for *psuché* here, by which it is translated in the two succeeding verses.

Except in this and another passage, where in quoting John 3 : 8, *pneuma* is translated, as in Luther's version, "Spirit" instead of "Wind," our authorized version has been always adhered to.—Tr.

own will, and fulfilleth God's will, his soul will be kept and preserved unto life eternal.

XXXV

How There Is Deep and True Humility and Poorness of Spirit In a Man Who Is "Made a Partaker of the Divine Nature"

Moreover, in a man who is "made a partaker of the divine nature," there is a thorough and deep humility, and where this is not, the man hath not been "made a partaker of the divine nature." So Christ taught in words and fulfilled in works. And this humility springeth up in the man, because in the true light he seeth (as it also really is) that substance, life, perceiving, knowledge, power, and what is thereof, do all belong to the True Good, and not to the creature; but that the creature of itself is nothing and hath nothing, and that when it turneth itself aside from the True Good in will or in works, nothing is left to it but pure evil. And therefore it is true to the very letter, that the creature, as creature, hath no worthiness in itself, and no right to anything, and no claim over any one, either over God or over the creature, and that it ought to give itself up to God and submit to him because that is just. And this is the chiefest and most weighty matter.

Now if we ought to be, and desire to be, obedient and submit unto God, we must also submit to what we receive at the hands of any of his creatures, or our submission is all false. From this latter article floweth true humility, as indeed it doth also from the former.[2] And unless this verily ought to be, and were wholly agreeable to God's justice, Christ would not have taught it in words, and fulfilled it in his life. And herein there is a veritable manifestation of God; and it is so of a truth, that of God's truth and justice this creature shall be subject to God and all creatures, and no thing or person shall be subject or obedient to her. God and all the creatures have a right over her and to her, but she hath a right to nothing: she is a debtor to all, and nothing is owing to her, so that she shall be ready to bear all things from others, and also if needs be to do all things for others. And out of this groweth that poorness of spirit which Christ said: "Blessed are the poor in spirit" (that is to say, the truly humble) "for their's is the kingdom of heaven." All this hath Christ taught in words and fulfilled with his life.

[2] Namely, God's having a right to our obedience.

XXXVI

How Nothing Is Contrary to God But Sin Only; and What Sin Is In Kind and Act

Further ye shall mark: when it is said that such a thing, or such a deed is contrary to God, or that such a thing is hateful to God, and grieveth his spirit, ye must know that no creature is contrary to God, or hateful or grievous unto him, in so far as it is, liveth, knoweth, hath power to do, or produce aught, and so forth, for all this is not contrary to God. That an evil spirit, or a man is, liveth, and the like, is altogether good and of God; for God is the Being of all that are, and the Life of all that live, and the Wisdom of all the wise; for all things have their being more truly in God than in themselves, and also their powers, knowledge, life, and the rest; for if it were not so, God would not be all good. And thus all creatures are good. Now what is good is agreeable to God and he will have it. Therefore it can not be contrary to him.

But what then is there which is contrary to God and hateful to him? Nothing but sin. But what is sin? Mark this: sin is nothing else than that the creature willeth otherwise than God willeth, and contrary to him. Each of us may see this in himself; for he who willeth otherwise than I, or whose will is contrary to mine, is my foe; but he who willeth the same as I, is my friend, and I love him. It is even so with God: and that is sin, and is contrary to God, and hateful and grievous to him. And he who willeth, speaketh, or is silent, doeth or leaveth undone, otherwise than as I will, is contrary to me, and an offense unto me. So it is also with God: when a man willeth otherwise than God, or contrary to God, whatever he doeth or leaveth undone, in short all that proceedeth from him, is contrary to God, and is sin. And whatsoever will willeth otherwise than God, is against God's will. As Christ said: "He who is not with me is against me." Hereby may each man see plainly whether or not he be without sin, and whether or not he be committing sin, and what sin is, and how sin ought to be atoned for, and wherewith it may be healed. And this contradiction to God's will is what we call, and is, disobedience. And therefore Adam, the I, the self, self-will, sin, or the old man, the turning aside or departing from God, do all mean one and the same thing.

[Chap. XXXVII. teaches how in God, as God, there can neither be Grief, Sorrow, Displeasure, nor the like, but how it is otherwise in a Man who is "made a Partaker of the Divine Nature."]

XXXVIII

How We Are to Put On the Life of Christ from Love, and Not for the Sake of Reward, and How We Must Never Grow Careless Concerning It, or Cast It Off

Now, wherever a man hath been made a partaker of the divine nature, in him is fulfilled the best and noblest life, and the worthiest in God's eyes, that hath been or can be. And of that eternal love which loveth goodness, as goodness and for the sake of goodness, a true, noble, Christ-like life is so greatly beloved that it will never be forsaken or cast off. Where a man hath tasted this life, it is impossible for him ever to part with it, were he to live until the judgment day. And tho he must die a thousand deaths, and tho all the sufferings that ever befell all creatures could be heaped upon him, he would rather undergo them all than fall away from this excellent life; and if he could exchange it for an angel's life, he would not.

This is our answer to the question, "if a man, by putting on Christ's life, can get nothing more than he hath already, and serve no end, what good will it do him?" This life is not chosen in order to serve any end, or to get anything by it, but for love of its nobleness, and because God loveth and esteemeth it so greatly. And whoever saith that he hath had enough of it, and may now lay it aside, hath never tasted nor known it; for he who hath truly felt or tasted it can never give it up again. And he who hath put on the life of Christ with the intent to win or deserve aught thereby hath taken it up as an hireling and not for love, and is altogether without it. For he who doth not take it up for love, hath none of it at all; he may dream indeed that he hath put it on, but he is deceived. Christ did not lead such a life as his for the sake of reward, but out of love; and love maketh such a life light and taketh away all its hardships, so that it becometh sweet and is gladly endured. But to him who hath not put it on from love, but hath done so, as he dreameth, for the sake of reward, it is utterly bitter and a weariness, and he would fain be quit of it. And it is a sure token of an hireling that he wisheth his work were at an end. But he who truly loveth it, is not offended at its toil nor suffering, nor the length of time it lasteth. Therefore it is written, "to serve God and live to him, is easy to him who doeth it." Truly it is so to him who doth it for love, but it is hard and wearisome to him who doth it for hire. It is the same with all virtue and good works, and likewise with order, laws, obedience to precepts, and the like. But God rejoiceth more over one man who truly loveth, than over a thousand hirelings.

A Prayer of Mary Carpenter

O Father, calm the turbulence of our passions; quiet the throbbing of our hopes; repress the waywardness of our wills; direct the motions of our affections; and sanctify the varieties of our lot. Be thou all in all to us; and may all things earthly, while we bend them to our growth in grace and to the work of blessing, dwell lightly in our hearts, so that we may readily, or even joyfully, give up whatever thou dost ask for. May we seek first thy kingdom and righteousness; resting assured that then all things needful shall be added unto us.

Father, pardon our past ingratitude and disobedience; and purify us, whether by thy gentler or thy sterner dealings, till we have done thy will on earth, and thou removest us to thine own presence with the redeemed in heaven. Amen.

SELECTIONS FROM

The Imitation of Christ

BY

THOMAS À KEMPIS

THOMAS À KEMPIS

German mystic and author of the well-known work, "The Imitation of Christ," was born at Kempen, near Düsseldorf, Germany, about 1380, and died near Zwolle in 1471. His paternal name was Hemerken, or Hämmerlein ("Little Hammer"). He was sent to the school at Deventer in 1395. This school was conducted by the Brethren of the Common Life. In 1399 he was admitted to the Augustinian convent of Mount Saint Agnes, near Zwolle. He received priest's orders in 1413, and was made sub-prior in 1429. His whole life appears to have been spent in the seclusion of the convent, where he lived to an extreme old age. It is said of him that he copied the Bible no less than four times. His writings are all of a devotional character, and include tracts, meditations, letters, sermons, and biographies. "The Imitation of Christ" "is a manual of devotion intended to help the soul in its communion with God and the pursuit of holiness. Its sentences are statements, not arguments, and are pitched in the highest key of Christian experience."

Of the Imitation of Christ, and Contempt of All the Vanities of the World

"He that followeth me, walketh not in darkness" (John 8:12), saith the Lord. These are the words of Christ, by which we are admonished how we ought to imitate his life and manners, if we will be truly enlightened, and be delivered from all blindness of heart.

Let therefore our chiefest endeavor be, to meditate upon the life of Jesus Christ.

2. The doctrine of Christ exceedeth all the doctrines of holy men; and he that hath the Spirit will find therein an hidden manna.

But it falleth out that many who often hear the gospel of Christ are yet but little affected, because they are void of the Spirit of Christ.

But whosoever would fully and feelingly understand the words of Christ must endeavor to conform his life wholly to the life of Christ.

3. What will it avail thee to dispute profoundly of the Trinity, if thou be void of humility, and art thereby displeasing to the Trinity?

Surely high words do not make a man holy and just; but a virtuous life maketh him dear to God.

Devotional Classics

I had rather feel compunction, than understand the definition thereof.

If thou didst know the whole Bible by heart, and the sayings of all the philosophers, what would all that profit thee without the love of God (1 Cor. 13 : 2) and without grace?

Vanity of vanities, and all is vanity (Eccles. 1 : 2), except to love God, and to serve him only.

This is the highest wisdom, by contempt of the world to tend toward the kingdom of heaven.

4. Vanity therefore it is to seek after perishing riches, and to trust in them.

It is also vanity to hunt after honors, and to climb to high degree.

It is vanity to follow the desires of the flesh, and to labor for that for which thou must afterward suffer grievous punishment.

Vanity it is, to wish to live long, and to be careless to live well.

It is vanity to mind only this present life, and not to foresee those things which are to come.

It is vanity to set thy love on that which speedily passeth away, and not to hasten thither where everlasting joy abideth.

5. Call often to mind that proverb, "The eye is not satisfied with seeing, nor the ear filled with hearing" (Eccles. 1 : 8).

Endeavor therefore to withdraw thy heart from the love of visible things, and to turn thyself to the invisible.

For they that follow their sensuality, do stain their own consciences, and lose the favor of God.

Of the Humble Conceit of Ourselves

All men naturally desire to know (Eccles. 1:13); but what availeth knowledge without the fear of God?

Surely, an humble husbandman that serveth God is better than a proud philosopher that neglecting himself laboreth to understand the course of the heavens.

Whoso knoweth himself well, groweth more mean in his own conceit, and delighteth not in the praises of men.

If I understood all things in the world, and were not in charity, what would that help me in the sight of God, who will judge me according to my deeds?

2. Cease from an inordinate desire of knowing, for therein is much distraction and deceit.

The learned are well-pleased to seem so to others, and to be accounted wise (1 Cor. 8:1).

There be many things, which to know doth little or nothing profit the soul:

And he is very unwise, that is intent upon other things than those that may avail him for his salvation.

Many words do not satisfy the soul; but a good life comforteth the mind, and a pure conscience giveth great assurance in the sight of God.

3. How much the more thou knowest, and how much the better thou understandest, so much the more grievously shalt thou therefore be judged, unless thy life be also more holy.

Be not therefore extolled in thine own mind for any art or science, but rather let the knowledge given thee make thee more humble and cautious.

If thou thinkest that thou understandest and knowest much; know also that there be many things more which thou knowest not.

Affect not to be overwise, but rather acknowledge thine own ignorance (Rom. 12: 16).

Why wilt thou prefer thyself before others, sith there be many more learned, and more skilful in the Scripture than thou art?

If thou wilt know or learn anything profitably, desire to be unknown and to be little esteemed.

4. The highest and most profitable reading is the true knowledge and consideration of ourselves.

Thomas à Kempis

It is great wisdom and perfection to esteem nothing of ourselves, and to think always well and highly of others.

If thou shouldst see another openly sin or commit some heinous offense, yet oughtest thou not to esteem the better of thyself; for thou knowest not how long thou shalt be able to remain in good estate.

We are all frail (Gen. 8:21), but thou oughtest to esteem none more frail than thyself.

Of the Doctrine of Truth

Happy is he whom truth by itself doth teach (Ps. 94:12), not by figures and words that pass away; but as it is in itself.

Our own opinion and our own sense do often deceive us, and they discern but little.

What availeth it to cavil and dispute much about dark and hidden things (Eccles. 3:9-11); whereas for being ignorant of them we shall not be so much as reproved at the day of judgment?

It is a great folly to neglect the things that are profitable and necessary, and give our minds to that which is curious and hurtful: we have eyes and see not (Ps. 115:5).

2. And what have we to do with *genus* and *species*, the dry notions of logicians?

He to whom the eternal word speaketh is

delivered from a world of unnecessary conceptions.

From that one Word are all things, and all speak that one; and this is the Beginning, which also speaketh unto us.

No man without that Word understandeth or judgeth rightly.

He to whom all things are one, he who reduceth all things to one, and seeth all things in one; may enjoy a quiet mind, and remain peaceable in God.

O God, who art the truth, make me one with thee in everlasting charity.

It is tedious to me often to read and hear many things: in thee is all that I would have and can desire.

Let all doctors hold their peace; let all creatures be silent in thy sight; speak thou alone unto me.

3. The more a man is united within himself, and becometh inwardly simple and pure, so much the more and higher things doth he understand without labor; for that he receiveth intellectual light from above (Matt. 11:25; Luke 10:21).

A pure, sincere, and stable spirit is not distracted, tho it be employed in many works; for that it works all to the honor of God, and inwardly being still and quiet, seeks not itself in anything it doth.

Who hinders and troubles thee more than the unmortified affections of thine own heart?

A good and godly man disposeth within himself beforehand those things which he is outwardly to act;

Neither do they draw him according to the desires of an inordinate inclination, but he ordereth them according to the prescript of right reason.

Who hath a greater combat than he that laboreth to overcome himself?

This ought to be our endeavor, to conquer ourselves, and daily to wax stronger, and to make a further growth in holiness.

4. All perfection in this life hath some imperfection mixed with it; and no knowledge of ours is without some darkness.

An humble knowledge of thyself is a surer way to God than a deep search after learning;

Yet learning is not to be blamed, nor the mere knowledge of anything whatsoever to be disliked, it being good in itself, and ordained by God; but a good conscience and a virtuous life is always to be preferred before it.

But because many endeavor rather to get knowledge than to live well; therefore they are often deceived, and reap either none or but little fruit.

5. O, if men bestowed as much labor in the

rooting out of vices and planting of virtues as they do in moving of questions, neither would there so much hurt be done, nor so great scandal be given in the world, nor so much looseness be practised in Religious Houses.

Truly, at the day of judgment we shall not be examined what we have read, but what we have done (Matt. 25); not how well we have spoken, but how religiously we have lived.

Tell me now, where are all those Doctors and Masters with whom thou wast well acquainted whilst they lived and flourished in learning?

Now others possess their livings and perhaps do scarce ever think of them. In their lifetime they seemed something, but now they are not spoken of.

6. O, how quickly doth the glory of the world pass away! (Eccles. 2:11). O that their life had been answerable to their learning! then had their study and reading been to good purpose.

How many perish by reason of vain learning (Titus 1:10) in this world, who take little care of the serving of God.

And because they rather choose to be great than humble, therefore they become vain in their imaginations (Rom. 1:21).

He is truly great that is great in charity.

Thomas a Kempis

He is truly great that is little in himself, and that maketh no account of any height of honor (Matt. 18:4; 23:11).

He is truly wise that accounteth all earthly things as dung, that he may gain Christ (Phil. 3:8).

And he is truly learned that doeth the will of God, and forsaketh his own will.

Of Wisdom and Forethought In Our Actions

We must not give ear to every saying or suggestion (1 John 4:1), but ought warily and leisurely to ponder things according to the will of God.

But alas! such is our weakness, that we often rather believe and speak evil of others than good.

Those that are perfect men do not easily give credit to everything one tells them; for they know that human frailty is prone to evil (Gen. 8:21), and very subject to fail in words (James 3:2).

2. It is great wisdom not to be rash in thy proceedings (Prov. 19:2) nor to stand stiffly in thine own conceits;

As also not to believe everything which thou hearest, not presently to relate again to others (Prov. 17:9) what thou hast heard or dost believe.

Consult with him that is wise and conscientious, and seek to be instructed by a better than thyself, rather than to follow thine own inventions (Prov. 12:15).

A good life maketh a man wise according to God (Prov. 15:33), and giveth him experience in many things (Eccles. 1:16).

The more humble a man is in himself, and the more subject unto God; so much the more prudent shall he be in all his affairs, and enjoy greater peace and quiet of heart.

Of the Reading of Holy Scriptures

Truth, not eloquence, is to be sought for in Holy Scripture.

Each part of the Scripture is to be read with the same Spirit wherewith it was written (Rom. 15:4).

We should rather search after our spiritual profit in the Scriptures, than subtlety of speech.

We ought to read plain and devout books as willingly as high and profound.

Let not the authority of the writer offend thee, whether he be of great or small learning; but let the love of pure truth draw thee to read (1 Cor. 2:4).

Search not who spoke this or that, but mark what is spoken.

2. Men pass away, but the truth of the Lord remaineth for ever (Ps. 117:2; Luke 21:33). God speaks unto us sundry ways without respect of persons (Rom. 2:11; 10:12; Col. 3:11).

Our own curiosity often hindereth us in reading of the Scriptures, when as we will examine and discuss that which we should rather pass over without more ado.

If thou desire to reap profit, read with humility, simplicity, and faithfulness; nor ever desire the estimation of learning.

Inquire willingly, and hear with silence the words of holy men; dislike not the parables of the elders, for they are not recounted without cause (Prov. 1:6; Eccles. 12:9).

Of Inordinate Affections

Whensoever a man desireth anything inordinately, he is presently disquieted in himself.

The proud and covetous can never rest. The poor and humble in spirit live together in all peace.

The man that is not yet perfectly dead to himself, is quickly tempted and overcome in small and trifling things.

The weak in spirit, and he that is yet in a manner carnal and prone to sensible things, can hardly withdraw himself altogether from earthly desires:

And therefore he is often afflicted, when he goeth about to withdraw himself from them; and easily falleth into indignation, when any opposition is made against him.

2. And if he hath followed therein his appetite, he is presently disquieted with remorse of conscience; for that he yielded to his passion, which profiteth him nothing to the obtaining of the peace he sought for.

True quietness of heart therefore is gotten by resisting our passions, not by obeying them.

There is then no peace in the heart of a carnal man, nor in him that is addicted to outward things, but in the spiritual and fervent man.

Of the Love of Solitude and Silence

Seek a convenient time (Eccles. 3:1) to retire into thyself, and meditate often upon God's loving kindness.

Meddle not with curiosities; but read such things as may rather yield compunction to thy heart, than occupation to thy head.

If thou wilt withdraw thyself from speaking vainly and from gadding idly, as also from hearkening after novelties and rumors, thou shalt find leisure enough and suitable for meditation on good things.

The greatest saints avoided the society of men (Heb. 11:38), when they could conveniently, and did rather choose to live in God, in secret.

2. One said, "As oft as I have been among men, I returned home less a man than I was before" (Seneca, Ep. vii).

And this we find true, when we talk long together. It is easier not to speak a word at all than not to speak more words than we should.

It is easier for a man to keep at home, than to keep himself well when he is abroad.

He therefore that intends to attain to the more inward and spiritual things of religion must with Jesus depart from the multitude and press of people (Matt. 5:1).

No man doth safely appear abroad, but he who gladly can abide at home, out of sight.

No man speaks securely, but he that holds his peace willingly (Eccles. 2:7).

No man ruleth safely, but he that is willingly ruled.

No man securely doth command, but he that hath learned readily to obey.

3. No man rejoiceth securely, unless he

hath within him the testimony of a good conscience.

And yet always the security of the saints was full of the fear of God.

Neither were they the less anxious and humble in themselves, for that they shined outwardly with grace and great virtues.

But the security of bad men ariseth from pride and presumption, and in the end it deceiveth them.

Altho thou seem to be a good religious man or a devout solitary, yet never promise thyself security in this life.

4. Oftentimes those who have been in the greatest esteem and account among men have fallen into the greatest danger by overmuch self-confidence.

Wherefore to many it is more profitable not to be altogether free from temptations, but to be often assaulted, lest they should be too secure, and so perhaps be puffed up with pride; or else too freely give themselves to worldly comforts.

O how good a conscience should he keep that would never seek after transitory joy nor ever entangle himself with the things of this world!

O how great peace and quietness should he possess that would cut off all vain anxiety, and think only upon divine things and such as are profitable for his soul, and would place all his confidence in God.

5. No man is worthy of heavenly comfort unless he have diligently exercised himself in holy compunction.

If thou desirest true contrition of heart, enter into thy secret chamber and shut out the tumults of the world, as it is written, "In your chambers be ye grieved" (Ps. 4:4, Vulgate). In thy chamber thou shalt find what abroad thou shalt too often lose.

The more thou visitest thy chamber, the more thou wilt like it; the less thou comest thereunto, the more thou wilt loath it. If in the beginning of thy conversion thou art content to remain in it, and keep to it well, it will afterward be to thee a dear friend, and a most pleasant comfort.

6. In silence and in stillness a religious soul advantageth herself, and learneth the mysteries of Holy Scripture.

There she findeth rivers of tears, wherein she may every night (Ps. 6:6) wash and cleanse herself; that she may be so much the more familiar with her Creator, by how much the farther off she liveth from all worldly disquiet.

Whoso therefore withdraweth himself from his acquaintance and friends, God will draw near unto him with his holy angels.

It is better for a man to live privately and to take care of himself than to neglect his soul, tho he could work wonders in the world.

It is commendable in a religious person seldom to go abroad, to be unwilling to see or to be seen.

7. Why art thou desirous to see that which it is unlawful for thee to have? The world passeth away and the lust thereof.

Our sensual desires draw us to rove abroad; but when the time is past, what carriest thou home with thee but a burdened conscience and distracted heart?

A merry going out bringeth often a mournful return home, and a joyful evening makes often a sad morning (Prov. 14:13).

So all carnal joy enters gently, but in the end it bites and stings to death.

What canst thou see elsewhere, which thou canst not see here? (Eccles. 1:10). Behold the heaven and the earth and all the elements; for of these are all things created.

8. What canst thou see anywhere that can long continue under the sun?

Thou thinkest perchance to satisfy thyself, but thou canst never attain it.

Shouldst thou see all things present before thine eyes, what were it but a vain sight? (Eccles. 3:11).

Lift up thine eyes (Ps. 121:1) to God in

the highest, and pray him to pardon thy sins and negligences.

Leave vain things to the vain; but be thou intent upon those things which God hath commanded thee.

Shut thy door upon thee (Matt. 6: 6), and call unto thee Jesus, thy Beloved.

Stay with him in thy closet; for thou shalt not find so great peace anywhere else.

If thou hadst not gone abroad and hearkened to idle rumors, thou wouldst the better have preserved a happy peace of mind. But since thou delightest some times to hear novelties, it is but fit that thou suffer for it some disquietude of heart.

Of the Inward Life

"The kingdom of God is within you" (Luke 17: 21), saith the Lord. Turn thee with thy whole heart (Joel 2: 12) unto the Lord, and forsake this wretched world, and thy soul shall find rest.

Learn to despise outward things and to give thyself to things inward, and thou shalt perceive the kingdom of God to come in thee.

"For the kingdom of God is peace and joy in the Holy Ghost" (Rom. 14: 17), which is not given to the unholy.

Christ will come unto thee and show thee his own consolation, if thou prepare for him a worthy mansion within thee.

All his glory and beauty is from within (Ps. 14:13), and there he delighteth himself.

The inward man he often visiteth; and hath with him sweet discourses, pleasant solace, much peace, familiarity exceeding wonderful.

2. O faithful soul, make ready thy heart for this Bridegroom, that he may vouchsafe to come unto thee, and to dwell within thee.

For thus saith he, "If any love me, he will keep my words, and we will come unto him, and will make our abode with him" (John 14:25).

Give therefore admittance unto Christ, and deny entrance to all others.

When thou hast Christ, thou art rich and hast enough. He will be thy faithful and provident helper in all things, so as thou shalt not need to trust in men.

For men soon change, and quickly fail; but Christ remaineth for ever (John 12:34), and standeth by us firmly unto the end.

3. There is no great trust to be put in a frail and mortal man (Jer. 17:5), even tho he be profitable and dear unto us; neither ought we to be much grieved, if some times he cross and contradict us.

They that to-day take thy part, to-morrow may be against thee; and often do they turn right round like the wind.

Put all thy trust in God (1 Pet. 5:7), let him be thy fear, and thy love; he shall answer for thee, and will do in all things what is best for thee.

Thou hast not here an abiding city (Heb. 13:14); and wheresoever thou mayest be, thou art a stranger and pilgrim: neither shalt thou ever have rest, unless thou be most inwardly united unto Christ.

4. Why dost thou here gaze about, since this is not the place of thy rest? In heaven ought to be thy home (Phil. 3:20), and all earthly things are to be looked upon as it were by the way.

All things pass away (Wisd. of Sol. 5:9), and thou together with them.

Beware thou cleave not unto them, lest thou be caught and so perish. Let thy thought be on the Highest, and thy prayer for mercy directed unto Christ without ceasing.

If thou canst not contemplate high and heavenly things, rest thyself in the passion of Christ, and dwell willingly in his sacred wounds.

For if thou fly devoutly unto the wounds and precious marks of the Lord Jesus, thou shalt feel great comfort in tribulation: neither wilt thou much care for the slights of men, and wilt easily bear words of detraction.

5. Christ was also in the world, despised of men and in greatest necessity, forsaken by his acquaintance and friends in the midst of slanders (Matt. 12:24; 16:21; John 15:20).

Christ was willing to suffer and be despised; and darest thou complain of any man?

Christ had adversaries and backbiters; and doest thou wish to have all men thy friends and benefactors?

Whence shall thy patience attain her crown (2 Tim. 2:5) if no adversity befall thee?

If thou art willing to suffer no opposition, how wilt thou be the friend of Christ?

Suffer with Christ and for Christ, if thou desire to reign with Christ.

6. If thou hadst but once perfectly entered into the secrets of the Lord Jesus, and tasted a little of his ardent love; then wouldst thou not regard thine own convenience or inconvenience, but rather wouldst rejoice at slanders, if they should be cast upon thee; for the love of Jesus maketh a man despise himself.

A lover of Jesus and of the truth, and a true inward Christian, and one free from inordinate affections, can freely turn himself unto God, and lift himself above himself in spirit, and with joy remain at rest.

7. He that judgeth of all things as they are, and not as they are said or esteemed to be, is truly wise, and taught rather of God than men (Isa. 54: 13).

He that can live inwardly, and make small reckoning of things without, neither requireth places nor expecteth times for performing of religious exercises.

A spiritual man quickly recollecteth himself, because he never poureth out himself wholly to outward things.

He is not hindered by outward labor or business, which may be necessary for the time: but as things fall out, so he accommodates himself to them.

He that is well ordered and disposed within himself, cares not for the strange and perverse behavior of men.

A man is hindered and distracted in proportion as he draweth external matters unto himself.

8. If it were well with thee, and thou wert well purified from sin, all things would fall out to thee for good (Rom. 8: 28), and to thy advancement.

But many things displease and often trouble thee; because thou art not yet perfectly dead unto thyself, nor separated from all earthly things.

Nothing so defileth and entangleth the heart of man as the impure love to creatures.

If thou refuse outward comfort, thou wilt be able to contemplate the things of heaven, and often to receive internal joy.

Of Humble Submission

Regard not much who is for thee or against thee (Rom. 8:31; 1 Cor. 4:3); but mind what thou art about, and take care that God may be with thee in everything thou doest.

Have a good conscience, and God will well defend thee (Ps. 28:7).

For whom God will help, no man's perverseness shall be able to hurt.

If thou canst be silent and suffer, without doubt thou shalt see that the Lord will help thee.

He knoweth the time and manner how to deliver thee, and therefore thou oughtest to resign thyself unto him.

It belongs to God to help, and to deliver from all confusion.

It is often very profitable, to keep us more humble, that others know and rebuke our faults.

2. When a man humbleth himself for his failings, then he easily pacifieth others, and

quickly satisfieth those that are offended with him.

God protecteth the humble and delivereth him (James 3, comp. 4:6; Job 5:11); the humble he loveth and comforteth; and unto the humble man he inclineth himself; unto the humble he giveth great grace; and after his humiliation he raiseth him to glory.

Unto the humble he revealeth his secrets (Matt. 11:25), and sweetly draweth and inviteth him unto himself.

The humble person, tho he suffer confusion, is yet tolerably well in peace; for that he resteth on God, and not on the world.

Do not think that thou hast made any progress, unless thou esteem thyself inferior to all.

Of a Good Peaceable Man

First, keep thyself in peace, and then shalt thou be able to pacify others.

A peaceable man doth more good than he that is well learned.

A passionate man draweth even good into evil, and easily believeth the worst.

A good peaceable man turneth all things to good.

He that is well in peace, is not suspicious of any (1 Cor. 13:15). But he that is discontented and troubled, is tossed with divers suspicions: he is neither quiet himself, nor suffereth others to be quiet.

He often speaketh that which he ought not to speak; and omitteth that which were more expedient for him to do.

He considereth what others are bound to do (Matt. 7:3), and neglecteth that which he is bound to himself.

First therefore have a careful zeal over thyself, and then thou mayest justly show thyself zealous also of thy neighbor's good.

2. Thou knowest well how to excuse and color thine own deeds, but thou art not willing to receive the excuses of others.

It were more just that thou shouldst accuse thyself, and excuse thy brother.

If thou will be borne withal, bear also with another (Gal. 6:2; 1 Cor. 13:7).

Behold, how far off thou art yet from true charity and humility; for that knows not how to be angry with any, or to be moved with indignation, but only against oneself.

It is no great matter to associate with the good and gentle; for this is naturally pleasing to all, and every one willingly enjoyeth peace, and loveth those best that agree with him.

But to be able to live peaceably with hard and perverse persons, or with the disorderly, or with such as go contrary to us, is a great grace, and a most commendable and manly thing.

3. Some there are that keep themselves in peace, and are in peace also with others.

And there are some that neither are in peace themselves, nor suffer others to be in peace: they are troublesome to others, but always more troublesome to themselves.

And others there are that keep themselves in peace, and study to bring others unto peace.

Nevertheless, our whole peace in this miserable life consisteth rather in humble sufferance than in not feeling adversities.

He that can best tell how to suffer will best keep himself in peace. That man is conqueror of himself and lord of the world, the friend of Christ, and heir of heaven.

Of a Pure Mind and Simple Intention

By two wings a man is lifted up from things earthly, namely, by simplicity and purity.

Simplicity ought to be in our intention; purity in our affections. Simplicity doth tend toward God; purity doth apprehend and taste him.

No good action will hinder thee, if thou be inwardly free from inordinate affection.

If thou intend and seek nothing else but the will of God and the good of thy neighbor, thou shalt thoroughly enjoy internal liberty.

If thy heart were sincere and upright, then every creature would be unto thee a looking-glass of life and a book of holy doctrine.

There is no creature so small and abject, that it representeth not the goodness of God (Rom. 1:20).

2. If thou wert inwardly good and pure (Prov. 3:3, 4; Ps. 119:100), then wouldst thou be able to see and understand all things well without impediment.

A pure heart penetrateth heaven and hell.

Such as every one is inwardly, so he judgeth outwardly.

If there be joy in the world, surely a man of a pure heart possesseth it.

And if there be any where tribulation and affliction, an evil conscience best knows it.

As iron put into the fire loseth its rust and becometh clearly red hot, so he that wholly turneth himself unto God puts off all sloth-fulness, and is transformed into a new man.

3. When a man beginneth to grow luke-warm, then he is afraid of a little labor, and willingly receiveth external comfort.

But when he once beginneth to overcome himself perfectly, and to walk manfully in the way of God; then he esteemeth those things to be light which before seemed grievous unto him.

Of the Consideration of Oneself

We can not trust much to ourselves (Jer. 17:5), because grace oftentimes is wanting to us, and understanding also.

There is but little light in us, and that which we have we quickly lose by our negligence.

Oftentimes, too, we do not perceive our own inward blindness how great it is.

We often do evil, and excuse it worse (Ps. 141:4).

We are sometimes moved with passion, and we think it to be zeal.

We reprehend small things in others, and pass over greater matters in ourselves (Matt. 7:5).

We quickly enough feel and weigh what we suffer at the hands of others; but we mind not what others suffer from us.

He that well and rightly considereth his own works, will find little cause to judge hardly of another.

2. The inward Christian preferreth the care of himself before all other cares (Matt. 16:26). And he that diligently attendeth

unto himself, can easily keep silence concerning others.

Thou wilt never be thus inwardly religious, unless thou pass over other men's matters with silence, and look especially to thyself.

If thou attend wholly unto God and thyself, thou wilt be but little moved with whatsoever thou seest abroad (1 Cor. 4:3; Gal. 1:10). Where art thou, when thou art not with thyself? And when thou hast run over all, what hast thou then profited, if thou hast neglected thyself.

If thou desirest peace of mind and true unity of purpose, thou must still put all things behind thee, and look only upon thyself.

3. Thou shalt then make great progress, if thou keep thyself free from all temporal care.

Thou shalt greatly fall back, if thou esteem temporal any thing.

Let nothing be great unto thee, nothing high, nothing pleasing, nothing acceptable, but only God himself, or that which is of God.

Esteem all comfort vain (Eccles. 1:14) which thou receivest from any creature.

A soul that loveth God, despiseth all things that are inferior unto God.

God alone is everlasting, and of infinite greatness, filling all creatures; the soul's solace, and the true joy of the heart.

Thomas a Kempis

Of the Joy of a Good Conscience

The glory of a good man, is the testimony of a good conscience (1 Cor. 1 : 31).

Have a good conscience, and thou shalt ever have joy.

A good conscience is able to bear very much, and is very cheerful in adversities.

An evil conscience is always fearful and unquiet (Wisd. of Sol. 17 : 11).

Thou shalt rest sweetly, if thy heart do not reprehend thee.

Never rejoice but when thou hast done well.

Sinners have never true joy, nor feel inward peace; because "There is no peace to the wicked," saith the Lord (Isa. 57 : 21).

And if they should say, "We are in peace, no evil shall fall upon us (Luke 12 : 19), and who shall dare to hurt us?" believe them not; for upon a sudden will arise the wrath of God, and their deeds shall be brought to naught, and their thoughts shall perish.

2. To glory in tribulation, is no hard thing for him that loveth; for so to glory, is to glory in the cross of the Lord.

That glory is short, which is given and received from men (John 5 : 44).

Sorrow always accompanieth the world's glory.

The glory of the good is in their consciences, and not in the tongues of men. The gladness of the just is of God (2 Cor. 3:5), and in God; and their joy is of the truth.

He that desireth true and everlasting glory, careth not for that which is temporal.

And he that seeketh temporal glory, or despiseth it not from his soul, showeth himself to have but little esteem of the glory of heaven.

He enjoyeth great tranquility of heart that careth neither for the praises nor dispraises of men.

3. He will easily be content and pacified whose conscience is pure.

Thou art not the more holy, tho thou be commended; nor the more worthless, tho thou be found fault with.

What thou art, that thou art; neither by words canst thou be made greater than what thou art in the sight of God.

If thou consider what thou art within thee, thou wilt not care what men talk of thee.

Man looketh on the countenance, but God on the heart (1 Sam. 16:7). Man considereth the deeds, but God weigheth the intentions.

To be always doing well, and to esteem little of oneself, is the sign of an humble soul.

To refuse to be comforted by any creature is a sign of great purity and inward confidence.

4. He that seeketh no witness for himself from without doth shew that he hath wholly committed himself unto God.

"For not he that commendeth himself, the same is approved (saith Saint Paul), but whom God commendeth" (2 Cor. 10:18).

To walk inwardly with God, and not to be kept abroad by any outward affection, is the state of a spiritual man.

Of the Love of Jesus Above All Things

Blessed is he that understandeth (Ps. 119: 1, 2) what it is to love Jesus, and to despise himself for Jesus' sake.

Thou oughtest to leave [thy] beloved, for [thy] Beloved (Deut. 6:5; Matt. 22:37); for that Jesus will be loved alone above all things.

The love of things created is deceitful and inconstant; the love of Jesus is faithful and persevering.

He that cleaveth unto creatures shall fall with that which is subject to fall; he that embraceth Jesus shall stand firmly for ever.

Love him, and keep him for thy friend, who when all go away will not forsake thee, nor suffer thee to perish in the end.

Some time or other thou must be separated from all, whether thou wilt or no.

2. Keep close to Jesus both in life and in death, and commit thyself unto his trust who, when all fail, can alone help thee.

Thy Beloved is of that nature that he will admit of no rival; but will have thy heart alone, and sit on his own throne as King.

If thou couldst empty thyself perfectly from all creatures, Jesus would willingly dwell with thee.

Whatsoever thou reposest in men, out of Jesus, is all little better than lost.

Trust not nor lean upon a reed full of wind; for that all flesh is grass, and all the glory thereof shall wither away as the flower of the field (Isa. 40:6).

3. Thou shalt quickly be deceived, if thou only look to the outward appearance of men.

For if in others thou seekest thy comfort and profit, thou shalt too often feel loss.

If thou seekest Jesus in all things, thou shalt surely find Jesus.

But if thou seekest thyself, thou shalt also find thyself, but to thine own destruction.

For man doth more hurt himself if he seek not Jesus, than the whole world and all his adversaries [could injure him].

Thomas a Kempis

Of Familiar Converse With Jesus

When Jesus is present, all is well, and nothing seems difficult; but when Jesus is absent, every thing is hard.

When Jesus speaks not inwardly to us, all other comfort is nothing worth; but if Jesus speak but one word, we feel great consolation.

Did not Mary Magdalene rise immediately from the place where she wept, when Martha said to her, "The Master is come, and calleth for thee?" (John 11:28).

Happy hour! when Jesus calleth from tears to spiritual joy.

How dry and hard art thou without Jesus! How foolish and vain, if thou desire any thing out of Jesus!

Is not this a greater loss than if thou shouldst lose the whole world? (Matt. 16:26).

2. What can the world profit thee without Jesus?

To be without Jesus is a grievous hell; and to be with Jesus, a sweet paradise.

If Jesus be with thee, no enemy shall be able to hurt thee (Rom. 8:35).

He that findeth Jesus findeth a good treasure (Matt. 13:44), yea, a Good above all good.

And he that loseth Jesus loseth much, indeed, yea, more than the whole world!

Most poor is he who liveth without Jesus (Luke 12:21); and he most rich who is well with Jesus.

3. It is a matter of great skill to know how to hold converse with Jesus; and to know how to keep Jesus, a point of great wisdom.

Be thou humble and peaceable, and Jesus will be with thee (Prov. 3:17).

Be devout and quiet, and Jesus will stay with thee.

Thou mayest soon drive away Jesus, and lose his favor, if thou wilt turn aside to outward things.

And if thou shouldst drive him from thee and lose him, unto whom wilt thou flee, and whom wilt thou then seek for thy friend?

Without a friend thou canst not well live; and if Jesus be not above all a friend to thee, thou shalt be indeed sad and desolate.

Thou actest therefore like an idiot, if thou trust or rejoice in any other (Gal. 6:14).

It is preferable to have all the world against us, rather than to have Jesus offended with us.

Amongst all therefore that be dear unto us, let Jesus alone be specially beloved.

4. Love all for Jesus, but Jesus for himself.

Jesus Christ alone is singularly to be beloved; who alone is found good and faithful above all friends.

For him, and in him, let as well friends as foes be dear unto thee; and all these are to be prayed for, that he would make them all to know and love him (Matt. 5:44; Luke 6: 27, 28).

Never desire to be singularly commended or beloved, for that appertaineth only unto God, who hath none like unto himself.

Neither do thou desire that the heart of any should be set on thee, nor do thou set thy heart on the love of any; but let Jesus be in thee, and in every good man.

5. Be pure and free within, and entangle not thy heart with any creature.

Thou oughtest to be naked and open before God, ever carrying thy heart pure toward him, if thou wouldst be free to consider and see how sweet the Lord is.

And truly, unless thou be prevented and drawn by his grace, thou shalt never attain to that happiness to forsake and take leave of all, that thou alone mayest be united to him alone.

For when the grace of God cometh unto a man, then he is made able for all things. And when it goeth away, then is he poor and weak, and as it were left only for the lash and scourge.

In this case thou oughtest not to be dejected, nor to despair; but at God's will to stand steadily, and whatever comes upon thee, to endure it for the glory of Jesus Christ; for after winter followeth summer, after night the day returneth, and after a tempest a great calm.

That All Our Hope and Trust Is to Be Fixt In God Alone

Lord, what is my confidence which I have in this life? or what is the greatest comfort I can derive from anything under heaven?

Is it not thou, O Lord my God, whose mercies are without number?

Where hath it ever been well with me without thee? or when could it be ill with me, when thou wert present?

I had rather be poor for thee, than rich without thee.

I rather choose to be a pilgrim on earth with thee, than without thee to possess heaven. Where thou art, there is heaven: and where thou art not, there is death and hell.

Thou art all my desire, and therefore I must needs sigh and call and earnestly pray unto thee.

In short, there is none whom I can fully trust to, none that can seasonably help me in my necessities, but only thou, my God.

Thou art my hope, thou my confidence;

thou art my Comforter, and in all things most
faithful unto me.

2. All men seek their own gain (Phil.
2:21); thou settest forward my salvation and
my profit only, and turnest all things to my
good.

Altho thou exposest me to divers temptations and adversities, yet thou orderest all
this to my advantage, who are wont to try thy
beloved ones a thousand ways.

In which trial of me thou oughtest no less
to be loved and praised than if thou didst fill
me full of heavenly consolations.

3. In thee therefore, O Lord God, I place
my whole hope and refuge; on thee I rest all
my tribulation and anguish; for I find all to
be weak and inconstant, whatsoever I behold
out of thee.

For many friends can not profit, nor strong
helpers assist, nor prudent counsellors give
a profitable answer, nor the books of the
learned afford comfort, nor any precious substance deliver, nor any place, however retired
and lovely, give shelter, unless thou thyself
dost assist, help, strengthen, console, instruct,
and guard us.

4. For all things that seem to belong to
the attainment of peace and felicity without
thee are nothing, and do bring in truth no
felicity at all.

Thou therefore art the fountain of all that is good, the Height of life, the Depth of all that can be spoken; and to hope in thee above all things, is the strongest comfort of thy servants.

To thee therefore do I lift up mine eyes; in thee, my God, the Father of mercies, do I put my trust.

Bless and sanctify my soul with thy heavenly blessings, that it may become thy holy habitation and the seat of thine eternal glory; and let nothing be found in this temple of thy divinity, which shall offend the eyes of thy majesty.

According to the greatness of thy goodness and multitude of thy mercies look upon me, and hear the prayer of thy poor servant, who is far exiled from thee in the land of the shadow of death.

Protect and keep the soul of me the meanest of thy servants, amidst so many dangers of this corruptible life, and by thy grace accompanying me direct it along the way of peace to its home of everlasting brightness. AMEN.

SELECTION FROM

A Treatise on Good Works

BY

MARTIN LUTHER

MARTIN LUTHER

Greatest of the Protestant reformers; born at
Eisleben, Germany, Nov. 10, 1483; died there Feb.
18, 1564. He was educated at Mansfield, Magde-
burg, Eisenach, and Erfurt; on July 17, 1505, he
entered the Augustinian monastery at Erfurt, and
in 1507 became priest. In 1508 he was appointed
professor of philosophy at Wittenburg; in 1511 he
went to Rome in the interests of his order, and on
his return (1512) received the doctorate of theology. His work as a reformer began over indulgences, and on Oct. 31, 1517, he nailed his ninety-
five theses on the castle church at Wittenburg,
"tho he had no intention of making a decisive
attack nor did he wish them to be generally cir-
culated." His theses spread throughout Germany,
as did his other writings, which called in question
the doctrine and authority of the Church. He
maintained that "the entire system of Christian
belief was to be derived not from the Fathers and
the Councils but from the Bible." His basic prin-
ciple was "justification by faith in Christ." Before
the Diet of Worms he refused to retract and later
was declared an outlaw. When he returned from
Worms he was seized at the instigation of his
friend, the Elector of Saxony, and safely lodged
in the old castle of the Wartburg, to save him from
the destruction which his conduct at Worms would
certainly have provoked. At Wartburg he began
his translation of the Bible, of which the New Testament was printed in September, 1522. Luther's
works are very voluminous, partly in Latin and
partly in German. Among those of more general
interest are his "Table-Talk," his "Letters," and
"Sermons." There are also his commentaries on
Galatians and Psalms, and he left thirty-eight
hymns, the most celebrated of which is his "battle
hymn," "Ein feste Burg ist unser Gott."

Faith As a Good Work

[The basis of the entire treatise is the Decalog. The part here reproduced discusses only the implications of the first commandment.]

1. We ought first to know that there are no good works except those which God has commanded, even as there is no sin except that which God has forbidden. Therefore whoever wishes to know and to do good works needs nothing else than to know God's commandments. Thus Christ says (Matt. 19), "If thou wilt enter into life, keep the commandments." And when the young man asks him (Matt. 19) what he shall do that he may inherit eternal life, Christ sets before him naught else but the ten commandments. Accordingly, we must learn how to distinguish among good works from the commandments of God, and not from the appearance, the magnitude, or the number of the works themselves, nor from the judgment of men or of human law or custom, as we see has been done and still is done because we are blind and despise the divine commandments.

2. The first and highest, the most precious, of all good works is faith in Christ, as he says

By kind permission of A. J. Holman & Co., Philadelphia.

(John 6). When the Jews asked him: "What shall we do that we may work the works of God?" he answered: "This is the work of God, that ye believe on him whom he hath sent." When we hear or preach this word, we hasten over it and deem it a very little thing and easy to do, whereas we ought here to pause a long time and to ponder it well. For in this work all good works must be done and receive from it the inflow of their goodness, like a loan. This we must put bluntly, that men may understand it.

We find many who pray, fast, establish endowments, do this or that, lead a good life before men, and yet if you should ask them whether they are sure that what they do pleases God they say, "No"; they do not know or they doubt. And there are some very learned men who mislead them and say that it is not necessary to be sure of this; and yet, on the other hand, these same men do nothing else but teach good works. Now all these works are done outside of faith, therefore they are nothing and altogether dead. For as their conscience stands toward God and as it believes, so also are the works which grow out of it. Now they have no faith, no good conscience toward God, therefore the works lack their head, and all their life and goodness is nothing. Hence it comes that when I exalt faith and reject such works done without faith, they accuse me of forbidding good works, when in truth I am trying hard to teach real good works of faith.

3. If you ask further whether they count it also a good work when they work at their trade, walk, stand, eat, drink, sleep, and do all kinds of works for the nourishment of the body or for the common welfare, and whether they believe that God takes pleasure in them because of such works, you will find that they say, "No"; and they define good works so narrowly that they are made to consist only of praying in church, fasting, and almsgiving. Other works they consider to be in vain, and think that God cares nothing for them. So through their damnable unbelief they curtail and lessen the service of God, who is served by all things whatsoever that are done, spoken, or thought in faith.

So teaches Ecclesiastes 9: "Go thy way with joy, eat and drink, and know that God accepteth thy works. Let thy garments be always white; and let thy head lack no ointment. Live joyfully with the wife whom thou lovest all the days of the life of thy vanity." "Let thy garments be always white," that is, let all our works be good, whatever they may be, without any distinction. And they are white when I am certain and believe that they please God. Then shall the head of my soul never lack the ointment of a joyful conscience.

So Christ says (John 8), "I do always those things that please him." And St. John says (1 John 3), "Hereby we know that we are of the truth, if we can comfort our hearts before him and have a good confidence. And if our heart condemns or frets us, God is greater than our heart, and we have confidence that whatsoever we ask we shall receive of him, because we keep his commandments and do those things that are pleasing in his sight." Again: "Whosoever is born of God (that is, whoever believes and trusts God), doth not commit sin, and can not sin." Again (Ps. 34): "None of them that trust in him shall do sin." And in Ps. 2, "Blessed are all they that put their trust in him." If this be true, then all that they do must be good, or the evil that they do must be quickly forgiven. Behold, then, why I exalt faith so greatly, draw all works into it, and reject all works which do not flow from it.

4. Now every one can note and tell for himself when he does what is good or what is not good; for if he finds his heart confident that it pleases God, the work is good, even if it were so small a thing as picking up a straw. If confidence is absent, or if he doubts, the work is not good, altho it should raise all the

dead and the man should give himself to be burned. This is the teaching of St. Paul (Rom. 14): "Whatsoever is not done of or in faith is sin." Faith, as the chief work, and no other work, has given us the name of "believers on Christ." For all other works a heathen . . . a sinner, may also do; but to trust firmly that he pleases God is possible only for a Christian who is enlightened and strengthened by grace.

That these words seem strange, and that some call me a heretic because of them, is due to the fact that men have followed blind reason and heathen ways, have set faith not above but beside other virtues, and have given it a work of its own, apart from all works of the other virtues; altho faith alone makes all other works good, acceptable, and worthy, in that it trusts God and does not doubt that for it all things that a man does are well done. Indeed, they have not let faith remain a work, but have made a *habitus*[1] of it, as they say, altho the Scripture gives the name of a good, divine work to no work except to faith alone. Therefore it is no wonder that they have become blind and leaders of the blind. And this faith brings with it at once love, peace, joy and hope. For God gives his Spirit at once to him who trusts him, as St. Paul says to the

---

[1] A quality, state, or condition, independent of works.

Galatians: "You received the Spirit not because of your good works, but when you believed the word of God."

5. In this faith all works become equal, and one is like the other; all distinctions between works fall away, whether they be great, small, short, long, few or many. For the works are acceptable not for their own sake, but because of the faith which alone is, works, and lives in each and every work without distinction, however numerous and various they are, just as all the members of the body live, work, and have their name from the head, and without the head no member can live, work, and have a name.

From which it further follows that a Christian who lives in this faith has no need of a teacher of good works, but whatever he finds to do he does, and all is well done; as Samuel said to Saul: "'The Spirit of the Lord will come upon thee and thou shalt be turned into another man; then do thou as occasion serves thee; for God is with thee." So also we read of St. Anna, Samuel's mother: " When she believed the priest Eli who promised her God's grace, she went home in joy and peace, and from that time no more turned hither and thither," that is, whatever occurred, it was all one to her. St. Paul also says: "Where the Spirit of Christ is, there all is free." For faith does not permit itself to be bound to any work, nor does it allow any work to be taken from it, but, as the first Psalm says, "He bringeth forth his fruit in his season," that is, as a matter of course.

6. This we may see in a common human example. When a man and a woman love, and are pleased with each other, and thoroughly believe in their love, who teaches them how they are to behave, what they are to do, leave undone, say, not say, think? Confidence alone teaches them all this and more. They make no difference in works; they do the great, the long, the much, as gladly as the small, the short, the little, and *vice versa;* and that, too, with joyful, peaceful, confident hearts, and each is a free companion of the other. But where there is a doubt, search is made for what is best; then a distinction of works is imagined whereby a man may win favor; and yet he goes about it with a heavy heart and great disrelish; he is, as it were, taken captive, more than half in despair, and often makes a fool of himself.

So a Christian who lives in this confidence toward God knows all things, can do all things, undertakes all things that are to be done, and does everything cheerfully and freely; not that he may gather many merits and good works, but because it is a pleasure for him to

please God thereby, and he serves God purely
for nothing, content that his service pleases
God. On the other hand, he who is not at one
with God, or doubts, hunts, and worries in
what way he may do enough and with many
works move God. He runs to St. James of
Compostella,[2] to Rome, to Jerusalem, hither
and yon, prays St. Bridget's[3] prayer and the
rest, fasts on this day and on that, makes confession here, and makes confession there, questions this man and that, and yet finds no peace.
He does all this with great effort, despair, and
disrelish of heart, so that the Scriptures rightly call such works in Hebrew *Avenamal,* that
is "labor and travail." And even then they
are not good works and are all lost. Many
have been crazed thereby; their fear has
brought them into all manner of misery. Of
these it is written (Wisd. of Sol. 5): "We
have wearied ourselves in the wrong way; and
have gone through deserts where there lay no

[2] St. Jacobi di Compostella, a place in Spain, where the
Apostle James, the son of Zebedee, who was killed in
Jerusalem (Acts 12:2), is in Spanish tradition said to
have died a martyr's death; since the ninth century a
noted and much-frequented goal of pilgrimages. The name
Compostella is a corruption of Giacomo Postolo, that is,
"James the Apostle."

[3] St. Bridget of Ireland, who died in 523, was con-
sidered a second Virgin Mary, the "Mary of the Irish."
Perhaps here confused with another Bridget, or Brigitta,
who died 1373, a Scottish saint, who wrote several
prayers, printed for the first time in 1492 and translated
into almost all European languages.

way; but as for the way of the Lord, we have not known it, and the sun of righteousness rose not upon us.''

7. In these works faith is still slight and weak; let us ask further whether they believe that they are well-pleasing to God when they suffer in body, property, honor, friends, or whatever they have, and believe that God of his mercy appoints their sufferings and difficulties for them, whether they be small or great. This is real strength, to trust in God when to all our senses and reason he appears to be angry; and to have greater confidence in him than we feel. Here he is hidden, as the bride says in the Song of Songs ''Behold he standeth behind our wall, he looketh forth at the windows''; that is, he stands hidden among the sufferings, which would separate us from him like a wall, yea, like a wall of stone, and yet he looks upon me and does not leave me, for he is standing and is ready graciously to help, and through the window of dim faith he permits himself to be seen. And Jeremiah says in Lamentations, ''He casts off men, but he does it not willingly.''

This faith they do not know at all, and give up, thinking that God has forsaken them and is become their enemy; they even lay the blame of their ills on men and devils, and have no confidence at all in God. For this reason, too, their suffering is always an offense and harmful to them, and yet they go and do some good works, as they think, and are not aware of their unbelief. But they who, in such suffering trust God and retain a good firm confidence in him, and believe that he is pleased with them, these see in their sufferings and afflictions nothing but precious merits and the rarest possessions, the value of which no one can estimate. For faith and confidence make precious before God all that which others think most shameful, so that it is written even of death in Ps. 116, "Precious in the sight of the Lord is the death of his saints." And just as the confidence and faith are better, higher, and stronger at this stage than in the first stage, so and to the same degree do the sufferings which are borne in this faith excel all works of faith. Therefore between such works and sufferings there is an immeasurable difference and the sufferings are infinitely better.

8. Beyond all this is the highest stage of faith, when God punishes the conscience not only with temporal sufferings, but with death, hell, and sin, and refuses grace and mercy as tho it were his will to condemn and to be angry eternally. This few men experience, but David cries out in Ps. 6, "O Lord, rebuke me not in thine anger." To believe at such

times that God, in his mercy, is pleased with us is the highest work that can be done by and in the creature,[4] but of this the work-righteous and doers of good works know nothing at all. For how could they here look for good things and grace from God, as long as they are not certain in their works and doubt even on the lowest step of faith.

In this way I have, as I said, always praised faith and rejected all works which are done without such faith, in order thereby to lead men from the false, pretentious, pharisaic, unbelieving good works, with which all monastic houses, churches, homes, low and higher classes are over-filled, and lead them to the true, genuine, thoroughly good, believing works. In this no one opposes me except the unclean beasts, which do not divide the hoof, as the law of Moses decrees; who will suffer no distinction among good works, but go lumbering along: if only they pray, fast, establish endowments, go to confession, and do enough, everything shall be good, altho in all this they have had no faith in God's grace and approval. Indeed, they consider the works best of all, when they have done many, great, and long works without any such confidence, and they look for good only after the works are done; and so they build their confidence not on

4 That is, by us men.

divine favor but on the works they have done,
that is on sand and water, from which they
must at last take a cruel fall, as Christ says
(Matt. 7). This good will and favor, on
which our confidence rests, was proclaimed by
the angels from heaven, when they sang on
Christmas night: "Glory to God in the highest, peace to earth, gracious favor to man."

• 9. Now this is the work of the first commandment, which commands: "Thou shalt
have no other gods," which means: "Since I
alone am God, thou shalt place all thy confidence, trust, and faith on me alone, and on
no one else." For that is not to have a God,
if you call him God only with your lips, or
worship him with the knees or bodily gestures;
but if you trust him with the heart, and look
to him for all good, grace, and favor, whether
in works or sufferings, in life or death, in joy
or sorrow; as the Lord Christ says to the
heathen woman (John 4): "I say unto thee,
they that worship God must worship him in
spirit and in truth." And this faith, faithfulness, confidence deep in the heart, is the
true fulfilling of the first commandment;
without this there is no other work that is able
to satisfy this commandment. And as this
commandment is the very first, highest, and
best, from which all the others proceed, in
which they exist, and by which they are direct-

ed and measured, so also its work, that is, the
faith and confidence in God's favor at all
times, is the very first, highest, and best,
from which all others must proceed, exist, remain, be directed and measured. Compared
with this, other works are just as if the other
commandments were without the first, and
there were no God. Therefore St. Augustine
well says that the works of the first commandment are faith, hope, and love. As I said
above, such faith and confidence bring hope
and love with them. Nay, if we see it aright,
love is the first, or comes at the same instant
with faith. For I could not trust God if I
did not think that he wished to be favorable
and to love me, which leads me, in turn, to
love him and to trust him heartily, and to look
to him for all good things.

10. Now you see for yourself that all those
who do not at all times trust God and do not
in all their works or sufferings, life and death,
trust in his favor, grace, and good-will, but
seek his favor in other things or in themselves,
do not keep this commandment, and practise
real idolatry, even if they were to do the works
of all the other commandments, and in addi-
tion had all the prayers, fasting, obedience,
patience, chastity, and innocence of all the
saints combined. For the chief work is not
present, without which all the others are noth-

ing but mere sham, show, and pretense, with
nothing back of them: against which Christ
warns us (Matt. 7): "Beware of false prophets, which come to you in sheep's clothing."
Such are all who wish with their many good
works, as they say, to make God favorable to
themselves, and to buy God's grace from him,
as if he were a huckster or a day-laborer, unwilling to give his grace and favor for nothing. These are the most perverse people on
earth, who will hardly or never be converted
to the right way. Such too are all who in adversity run hither and thither, and look for
counsel and help everywhere except from God,
from whom they are most urgently commanded
to seek it; whom the Prophet Isaiah reproves
thus (Chap. 9): "The mad people turneth not
unto him that smiteth them": that is, God
smote them and sent them sufferings and all
kinds of adversity, that they should run to
him and trust him. But they ran away from
him to men, now to Egypt, now to Assyria,
perchance also to the devil; and of such idolatry much is written in the same prophet and
in the books of the Kings. This is also the
way of all holy hypocrites when they are in
trouble: they do not run to God, but flee from
him, and only think of how they may get rid
of their trouble through their own efforts or
through human help, and yet they consider

themselves and let others consider them pious people.

11. This is what St. Paul means in many places, where he ascribes so much to faith, that he says: "The righteous man draws his life out of his faith," and faith is that because of which he is counted righteous before God. If righteousness consists of faith, it is clear that faith fulfils all commandments and makes all works righteous, since no one is justified except he keep all the commands of God. Again, the works can justify no one before God without faith. So utterly and roundly does the apostle reject works and praise faith that some have taken offense at his words and say: "Well then, we will do no more good works," altho he condemns such men as erring and foolish.

So men still do. When we reject the great, pretentious works of our time, which are done entirely without faith, they say: Men are only to believe and not to do anything good. For nowadays they say that the works of the first commandment are singing, reading, organ-playing, reading the mass, saying matins and vespers and the other hours, the founding and decorating of churches, altars, and monastic houses, the gathering of bells, jewels, garments, trinkets and treasures, running to Rome and to the saints. Further, when we are drest up and bow, kneel, pray the rosary and the psalter, and all this not before an idol, but before the holy cross of God or the pictures of his saints: this we call honoring and worshiping God, and, according to the first commandment, "Having no other gods"; altho these things usurers, adulterers, and all manner of sinners can do too, and do them daily.

Of course, if these things are done with such faith that we believe that they please God, then they are praiseworthy, not because of their virtue, but because of such faith, for which all works are of equal value, as has been said. But if we doubt or do not believe that God is gracious to us and is pleased with us, or if we presumptuously expect to please him only through and after our works, then it is all pure deception, outwardly honoring God but inwardly setting up self as a false God. This is the reason why I have so often spoken against the display, magnificence and multitude of such works and have rejected them, because it is as clear as day that they are not only done in doubt or without faith, but there is not one in a thousand who does not set his confidence upon the works, expecting by them to win God's favor and anticipate his grace; and so they make a fair[5] of them, a thing

---

[5] A *Jahrmarkt;* the reference here being to the bargaining common at such yearly fairs.

which God can not endure, since he has promised his grace freely, and wills that we begin by trusting that grace, and in it perform all works, whatever they may be.

12. Note for yourself, then, how far apart these two are: keeping the first commandment with outward works only, and keeping it with inward trust. For this last makes true, living children of God, the other only makes worse idolatry and the most mischievous hypocrites on earth, who with their apparent righteousness lead unnumbered people into their way, and yet allow them to be without faith, so that they are miserably misled, and are caught in the pitiable babbling and mummery. Of such Christ says (Matt. 24): "Beware, if any man shall say to you, Lo, here is Christ, or there"; and (John 4): "I say unto thee, the hour cometh, when ye shall neither in this mountain nor yet at Jerusalem worship God, for the Father seeketh spiritual worshipers."

These and similar passages have moved me and ought to move everyone to reject the great display of bulls, seals, flags, indulgences, by which the poor folk are led to build churches, to give, to endow, to pray, and yet faith is not mentioned, and is even supprest. For since faith knows no distinction among works, such exaltation and urging of one work above another can not exist beside faith. For faith desires to be the only service of God, and will grant this name and honor to no other work, except in so far as faith imparts it, as it does when the work is done in faith and by faith. This perversion is indicated in the Old Testament, when the Jews left the temple and sacrificed at other places, in the green parks and on the mountains. This is what these men also do: They are zealous to do all works, but this chief work of faith they regard not at all.

13. Where now are they who ask, what works are good; what they shall do; how they shall be religious? Yes, and where are they who say that when we preach of faith, we shall neither teach nor do works? Does not this first commandment give us more work to do than any man can do? If a man were a thousand men, or all men, or all creatures, this commandment would yet ask enough of him, and more than enough, since he is commanded to live and walk at all times in faith and confidence toward God, to place such faith in no one else, and so to have only one, the true God and none other.

Now, since the being and nature of man cannot for an instant be without doing or not doing something, enduring or running away from something (for, as we see, life never rests), let him who will be pious and filled

with good works begin and in all his life and
works at all times exercise himself in this
faith; let him learn to do and to leave undone
all things in such continual faith, then will
he find how much work he has to do, and how
completely all things are included in faith;
how he dare never grow idle, because his very
idling must be the exercise and work of faith.
In brief, nothing can be in or about us and
nothing can happen to us but that it must be
good and meritorious, if we believe (as we
ought) that all things please God. So says
St. Paul: "Dear brethren, all that ye do,
whether ye eat or drink, do all in the name
of Jesus Christ, our Lord." Now it can not
be done in this name except it be done in this
faith. Likewise (Rom. 8): "We know that
all things work together for good to the saints
of God."

Therefore, when some say that good works
are forbidden when we preach faith alone, it
is as if I said to a sick man: "If you had
health, you would have the use of all your
limbs; but without health, the works of all
your limbs are nothing"; and he wanted to
infer that I had forbidden the works of all
his limbs; whereas, on the contrary, I meant
that he must first have health, which will
work all the works of all the members. So
faith also must be in all works the master-

workman and captain, or they are nothing at all.

14. You might say: "Why then do we have so many laws of the Church and of the State, and many ceremonies of churches, monastic houses, holy places, which urge and tempt men to good works, if faith does all things through the first commandment? I answer: Simply because we do not all have faith or do not heed it. If every man had faith, we would need no more laws, but every one would of himself at all times do good works, as his confidence in God teaches him.

But now there are four kinds of men: the first, just mentioned, who need no law, of whom St. Paul says (1 Tim. 1): "The law is not made for a righteous man," that is, for the believer, but believers of themselves do what they know and can do, only because they firmly trust that God's favor and grace rests upon them in all things. The second class want to abuse this freedom, put a false confidence in it, and grow lazy; of whom St. Peter says (1 Peter 2): "Ye shall live as free men, but not using your liberty for a cloak of maliciousness," as if he said: The freedom of faith does not permit sins, nor will it cover them, but it sets us free to do all manner of good works and to endure all things as they happen to us, so that a man is not bound only to one work or to a few. So also St. Paul (Gal. 5): "Use not your liberty for an occasion to the flesh." Such men must be urged by laws and hemmed in by teaching and exhortation. The third class are wicked men, always ready for sins; these must be constrained by spiritual and temporal laws, like wild horses and dogs, and where this does not help, they must be put to death by the worldly sword, as St. Paul says (Rom. 13): "The worldly ruler bears the sword, and serves God with it, not as a terror to the good, but to the evil." The fourth class, who are still lusty and childish in their understanding of faith and of the spiritual life, must be coaxed like young children and tempted with external, definite, and prescribed decorations, with reading, praying, fasting, singing, adorning of churches, organ-playing, and such other things as are commanded and observed in monastic houses and churches, until they also learn to know the faith. Altho there is great danger here, when the rulers, as is now, alas! the case, busy themselves with and insist upon such ceremonies and external works as if they were the true works, and neglect faith, which they ought always to teach along with these works, just as a mother gives her child other food along with the milk, until the child can eat the strong food by itself.

15. Since, then, we are not all alike, we must tolerate such people, share their observances and burdens, and not despise them, but teach them the true way of faith. So St. Paul teaches (Rom. 14): "Him that is weak in the faith receive ye, to teach him." And so he did himself (1 Cor. 9): "To them that are under the law, I became as under the law, altho I was not under the law." And Christ (Matt. 17), when he was asked to pay tribute, which he was not obliged to pay, argues with St. Peter, whether the children of kings must give tribute, or only other people. St. Peter answers: "Only other people." Christ said: "Then are the children of kings free; notwithstanding, lest we should offend them, go thou to the sea, and cast an hook, and take up the fish that first cometh up; and in his mouth thou shalt find a piece of money; take that and give it for me and thee."

Here we see that all works and things are free to a Christian through his faith: and yet, because the others do not yet believe, he observes and bears with them what he is not obligated to do. But this he does freely, for he is certain that this is pleasing to God, and he does it willingly, accepts it as any other free work which comes to his hand without his choice, because he desires and seeks no more than that he may in his faith do works to please God.

But since in this discourse we have undertaken to teach what righteous and good works are, and are now speaking of the highest work, it is clear that we do not speak of the second, third, and fourth classes of men, but of the first, into whose likeness all the others are to grow, and until they do so the first class must endure and instruct them. Therefore we must not despise, as if they were hopeless, these men of weak faith, who would gladly do right and learn, and yet can not understand because of the ceremonies to which they cling; we must rather blame their ignorant, blind teachers, who have never taught them the faith, and have led them so deeply into works. They must be gently and gradually led back again to faith, as a sick man is treated, and must be allowed for a time, for their conscience sake, to cling to some works and do them as necessary to salvation, so long as they rightly grasp the faith; lest if we try to tear them out so suddenly, their weak consciences be quite shattered and confused and retain neither faith nor works. But the hard-headed, who, hardened in their works, give no heed to what is said of faith and fight against it, these we must, as Christ did and taught, let go their way, that the blind may lead the blind.

16. But you say: How can I trust surely that all my works are pleasing to God, when

at times I fall, and talk, eat, drink and sleep too much, or otherwise trangress, as I can not help doing? Answer: This question shows that you still regard faith as a work among other works, and do not set it above all works. For it is the highest work for this very reason, because it remains and blots out these daily sins by not doubting that God is so kind to you as to wink at such daily transgression and weakness. Aye, even if a deadly sin should occur (which, however, never or rarely happens to those who live in faith and trust toward God), yet faith rises again and does not doubt that its sin is already gone; as it is written (1 John 2): "My little children, these things I write unto you, that ye sin not. And if any man sin, we have an Advocate with God the Father, Jesus Christ, who is the propitiation of all our sins." And (Wisd. of Sol. 15): "For if we sin, we are thine, knowing thy power," and (Prov. 24): "For a just man falleth seven times, and riseth up again." Yes, this confidence and faith must be so high and strong that the man knows that all his life and works are nothing but damnable sins before God's judgment, as it is written (Ps. 143): "In thy sight shall no man living be justified"; and he must entirely despair of his works, believing that they can not be good except through this faith,

which looks for no judgment, but only for
pure grace, favor, kindness, and mercy, like
David (Ps. 26): "Thy loving-kindness is ever
before mine eyes, and I have trusted in thy
truth" (Ps. 4): "The light of thy countenance
is lift up upon us (that is, the knowledge of
thy grace through faith), and thereby hast
thou put gladness in my heart"; for as faith
trusts, so it receives.

See, thus are works forgiven, are without
guilt and are good, not by their own nature
but by the mercy and grace of God, because
of the faith which trusts on the mercy of God.
Therefore we must fear because of the works,
but comfort ourselves because of the grace of
God, as it is written (Ps. 147): "The Lord
taketh pleasure in them that fear him, in those
that hope in his mercy." So we pray with
perfect confidence, "Our Father," and yet
petition: "Forgive us our trespasses"; we are
children and yet sinners; are acceptable and
yet do not do enough; and all this is the
work of faith, firmly grounded in God's grace.

17. But if you ask, where the faith and the
confidence can be found and whence they
come, this it is certainly most necessary to
know. First: without doubt faith does not
come from your works or merit, but alone
from Jesus Christ, and is freely promised and
given; as St. Paul writes (Rom. 5): "God

commendeth his love to us as exceeding sweet and kindly, in that, while we were yet sinners, Christ died for us''; as if he said: ''Ought not this give us a strong, unconquerable confidence, that before we prayed or cared for it, yes, while we still continually walked in sins, Christ died for our sin?'' St. Paul concludes: ''If while we were yet sinners Christ died for us, how much more then, being justified by his blood, shall we be saved from wrath through him; and if, when we were enemies, we were reconciled to God by the death of his Son, much more, being reconciled, shall we be saved by his Life.''

Lo! thus must thou form Christ within thyself and see how in him God holds before thee and offers thee his mercy without any previous merits of thine own, and from such a view of his grace must thou draw faith and confidence of the forgiveness of all thy sins. Faith, therefore, does not begin with works, neither do they create it, but it must spring up and flow from the blood, wounds, and death of Christ. If thou see in these that God is so kindly affectioned toward thee that he gives even his Son for thee, then thy heart must also in its turn grow sweet and kindly affectioned toward God, and so thy confidence must grow out of pure goodwill and love—God's love toward thee

and thine toward God. We never read that
the Holy Spirit was given to any one when he
did works, but always when men have heard
the gospel of Christ and the mercy of God.
From this same Word and from no other
source must faith still come, even in our day
and always. For Christ is the rock out of
which men suck oil and honey, as Moses says
(Deut. 32).

A Prayer of Robert Louis Stevenson

We beseech thee, Lord, to behold us with
favor, folk of many families and nations
gathered together in the peace of this roof,
weak men and women, subsisting under the
covert of thy patience. Be patient still; suffer us yet a while longer—with our broken
purposes of good, with our idle endeavors
against evil, suffer us a while longer to endure and (if it may be) help us to do better.
Bless to us our extraordinary mercies; if the
day come when these must be taken, brace us
to play the man under affliction. Be with our
friends, be with ourselves. Go with each of
us to rest; if any awake, temper to them the
dark hours of watching; and when the day re-

turns, return to us our sun and comforter and call us up with morning faces and with morning hearts eager to labor; eager to be happy, if happiness shall be our portion; and if the day be marked for sorrow, strong to endure it. AMEN.

A Prayer of Gerhard Tersteegen

O Lord, thy hands have formed us, and thou hast sent us into this world, that we may walk in the way that leads to heaven and thyself and may find a lasting rest in thee who art the source and center of our souls. Look in pity on us poor pilgrims in the narrow way; let us not go astray, but reach at last our true home where our Father dwells. Guide and govern us from day to day, and bestow on us food and strength for body and soul, that we may journey on in peace. Forgive us for having hitherto so often wavered or looked back, and let us henceforth march straight on in the way of thy laws, and may our last step be a safe and peaceful passage to the arms of thy love, and the blessed fellowship of the saints in light. Hear us, O Lord, and glorify thy name in us that we may glorify thee for ever and ever. AMEN.

SELECTIONS FROM

Spiritual Exercises

BY

IGNATIUS OF LOYOLA

From the Translation

BY

JOHN MORRIS, S.J.

IGNATIUS OF LOYOLA

Founder of the Jesuit order; born at the castle of Loyola, near Azpeitia in the province of Guipuzcoa, Spain, probably Christmas night, 1491; died at Rome, July 31, 1556. After serving as a page at the court of Ferdinand he became a soldier and was severely wounded at the battle of Pampeluna. During this period of suffering he read the lives of the saints and became fired with an ambition to follow Christ "in a life of self-denying labor, and to emulate the heroic deeds of Francis of Assisi, Dominic, and other great monastic leaders." On March 25, 1522, he hung his military accoutrements before tne image of the Virgin in the Dominican monastery of Montserrat. He soon entered the monastery of Manresa, becoming a rigorous ascetic. In 1523 he left Manresa for Jerusalem, where he journeyed without money or supplies, and returned to Venice January, 1524, convinced that he could accomplish little without scholastic training. He then went to Barcelona and took his place (tho thirty-three years old) among the school-boys to learn the rudiments of Latin. In two years he was able to enter the University of Alcala, and in the autumn of 1527 removed to the University of Salamanca. At both universities he incurred the censure of the authorities through his efforts to win converts among the students by inducing them to subject themselves to courses of training in the "Spiritual Exercises." Early in 1528 he entered the University of Paris, where he remained over seven years, perfecting his literary and theological education. His tract "On the Virtue of Obedience" and his "Spiritual Exercises" best set forth the spirit of the man.

First Principle and Foundation

Man was created to praise, reverence, and serve God our Lord, and by this means to save his soul; and the other things on the face of the earth were created for man's sake, and in order to aid him in the prosecution of the end for which he was created. Whence it follows that man must make use of them in so far as they help him to attain his end, and in the same way he ought to withdraw himself from them in so far as they hinder him from it. It is therefore necessary that we should make ourselves indifferent to all created things, in so far as it is left to the liberty of our free-will to do so, and is not forbidden; in such sort that we do not for our part wish for health rather than sickness, for wealth rather than poverty, for honor rather than dishonor, for a long life rather than a short one; and so in all other things, desiring and choosing only those which most lead us to the end for which we were created.

Contemplation For Obtaining Love

Two things are to be noticed here:
The first is, that love ought to be found in

deeds rather than words. The second is, that love consists in mutual interchange on either side; that is to say, in the lover giving and communicating with the beloved what he has or can give, and on the other hand, in the beloved sharing with the lover, so that if the one have knowledge, honor, riches, he share it with him who has them not, and thus the one share all with the other.

The usual preparatory prayer [is to be employed].

The first prelude is a composition of place, and it is here to see myself standing before God our Lord and his angels and saints who are interceding for me.

The second prelude is to ask for what I want. It will be here to ask for an interior knowledge of the many and great benefits I have received, that, thoroughly grateful, I may in all things love and serve his divine Majesty.

The first point is to call to mind the benefits received, of my creation, redemption, and particular gifts, dwelling with great affection on how much God our Lord has done for me, and how much he has given me of that which he has; and consequently, how much he desires to give me himself in so far as he can according to his divine ordinance; and then to reflect in myself what I, on my side, with great reason and justice, ought to offer and give to his divine Majesty, that is to say, all things that are mine, and myself with them, saying, as one who makes an offering, with great affection:

"Take, O Lord, and receive all my liberty, my memory, my understanding, and all my will, whatsoever I have and possess. Thou hast given all these things to me; to thee, O Lord, I restore them: all art thine, dispose of them all according to thy will. Give me thy love and thy grace, for this is enough for me."

The second point is to consider how God dwells in creatures, in the elements giving them being, in the plants giving them growth, in animals giving them feeling, and in men giving them understanding, and so in me giving me being, life, feeling, and causing me to understand; making likewise of me a temple, since I am created to the likeness and image of his divine Majesty; and then reflecting on myself in the same way as has been said in the first point, or in any other way that I shall feel to be better. And let the same be done with regard to each of the following points.

The third point is to consider how God works and labors for me in all created things on the face of the earth, that is, he behaves like one that labors, as in the heavens, elements, plants, fruit, cattle, etc., giving them being, preserving them, giving them growth and feeling, etc., and then to reflect on myself.

The fourth point is to see how all good things and all gifts descend from above, such as my limited power from the supreme and infinite Might on high, and in the same way, justice, goodness, pity, mercy, etc., just as the rays descend from the sun, and waters from the spring. Then to conclude by reflecting on myself, as has been said before.

Rules For the Discernment of Spirits

Rules for in some degree perceiving and knowing the various motions excited in the soul; the good, that they may be admitted; the bad, that they may be rejected.

1. In the case of those who go from mortal sin to mortal sin, the enemy is generally wont to place before their eyes apparent pleasures, causing them to imagine sensual gratifications and pleasures, in order to keep them fast and to plunge them deeper in their vices and sins. The good Spirit in such persons acts in the contrary manner, causing them to feel the stings and the remorse of conscience by the reproaches of reason.

2. In those who go on earnestly rooting out

their sins, and advancing daily from good to better in the service of God our Lord, the contrary to what is set down in the first rule takes place; for now it belongs to the evil spirit to cause anxiety and sadness, and to place obstacles in the way, disquieting the soul by false reasons, so that it make no further progress; and it belongs to the good Spirit to inspire it with courage and strength, to give it consolation, tears, inspirations, and peace, making things easy, and removing every impediment, that it may make progress in good works.

3. On Spiritual Consolation.—I call it consolation when there is excited in the soul some interior motion by which it begins to be inflamed with the love of its Creator and Lord, and when, consequently, it can love no created thing on the face of the earth in itself, but only in the Creator of them all. Likewise, when it sheds tears, moving it to the love of its Lord, whether it be from grief for its sins, or from the passion of Christ our Lord, or from other things directly ordained to his service and praise. Finally, I call consolation every increase of hope, faith, and charity, and all interior joy, which calls and attracts man to heavenly things and to the salvation of his own soul, rendering it quiet and tranquil in its Creator and Lord.

4. On Spiritual Desolation.—I call desolation all that is contrary to what is set down in the third rule, as darkness and disquiet of soul, an attraction toward low and earthly objects, the disquiet of various agitations and temptations, which move it to diffidence, without hope and without love, when the soul finds itself slothful, tepid, sad, and, as it were, separated from its Creator and Lord. For as consolation is contrary to desolation, so the thoughts that spring from consolation are contrary to those that spring from desolation.

5. In time of desolation we must never make a change, but remain firm and constant in the resolutions and determination made on the day preceding this desolation, or in the preceding consolation. For as in consolation it is the good Spirit that guides and directs us, so in desolation it is the bad spirit, by whose counsels we can not find the way to any right decision:

6. Altho in desolation we ought not to change our former resolutions, it is very profitable vehemently to make change in ourselves in ways that oppose the desolation; as, for example, by insisting more on prayer and meditation, by frequent examination, and by increasing in some suitable manner our penances.

7. Let him who is in desolation consider

how our Lord, to try him, has left him to his natural powers, that he may resist the various agitations and temptations of the enemy; and to do so is always in his power, by the assistance of God, which always remains to him, tho he may not clearly perceive it, as our Lord has withdrawn from him his great favor, great love, and intense grace, leaving him, however, grace sufficient for his eternal salvation.

8. Let him who is in desolation strive to remain in patience, a virtue contrary to the troubles which harass him; and let him think he will shortly be consoled, using all endeavors against the desolation in the way explained in the sixth rule.

9. There are three principal reasons why we find ourselves in desolation. The first is because we are lukewarm, slothful, or negligent in our spiritual exercises, and thus on account of our faults spiritual consolation is removed from us. The second reason is that God may try how much we are worth, and how much we progress in his service and praise when deprived of such a bountiful pay, as it were, of consolations and special graces. The third reason is that he may give us a true knowledge whereby we may intimately feel that it is not in our power to acquire or retain great devotion, ardent love, tears, or any

other spiritual consolation, but that all is a
gift and favor of God our Lord, and to teach
us not to build our nest in another's house,
by allowing our intellect to be lifted up to
any kind of pride or vainglory, by attributing
to ourselves feelings of devotion or other kinds
of spiritual consolation.

10. Let him who is in consolation think
how he will be in future desolation, gaining
fresh strength for it.

11. Let him who is in consolation strive
to humble and lower himself as far as he can,
thinking how little he is worth in time of
desolation without such a grace or consolation; on the other hand he who is in desolation must remember that he can do much
with sufficient grace to resist all his enemies,
when he takes strength in his Creator and
Lord.

12. The enemy acts like a woman, inasmuch as he is weak in spite of himself, but
strong in will; for as it is in the nature
of a woman, quarreling with a man, to lose
courage and to take to flight when he shows
himself undaunted; and on the contrary, if
the man begin to take to flight and to lose
courage, the rage, the spite, and the ferocity
of the woman become very great, and altogether without bounds: so in the same manner it is in the nature of our enemy to become

powerless and to lose courage (while his temptations take to flight), when the person who is exercising himself in spiritual matters shows a dauntless front to the temptations of the enemy, acting in a manner diametrically opposed to them; and on the contrary, if the exercitant begins to fear and to lose courage in sustaining temptation, there is no beast so fierce on the face of the earth as the enemy of our human nature in prosecuting with intense malice his wicked designs.

13. He also acts like a false lover, inasmuch as he wishes to remain hidden and undiscovered; for as this false man, speaking with an evil purpose, and paying court to the daughter of some honest father or the wife of some honest man, wishes his conversations and insinuations to be kept secret, and, on the contrary, is much displeased when the daughter discovers to her father, or the wife to her husband, his deceitful words and his depraved intention, because he easily infers that he can not succeed in the designs he has conceived; in the same way, when the enemy of our human nature obtrudes on a just soul his wiles and deceits, he wishes and desires that they be furtively received and kept secret, but he is very displeased when they are discovered to a good confessor or some other spiritual person who knows his frauds and

malice, because he infers that he can not succeed in the wicked design he had conceived, as his evident frauds are laid open.

14. He acts likewise as a military chief does in order to get possession of and to despoil the object of his desires. For as a leader and general, pitching his camp, and inspecting the strength and condition of some citadel, storms it on the weakest side; in the same way the enemy of our human nature prowls round and explores on all sides all our virtues, theological, cardinal, and moral, and where he finds us weakest, and in greatest need as regards our eternal salvation, there he makes his attack, and strives to take us by storm.

Further Rules to the Same Effect

1. It belongs to God and his angels to give in their motions true joy and spiritual gladness, removing all sadness and disturbance of mind occasioned by the enemy; while it belongs to him to fight against such joy and spiritual consolation, bringing forward pretended reasons, sophistries, and perpetual fallacies.

2. It belongs to God our Lord alone to grant consolation to the soul without any preceding cause for it, because it belongs to

the Creator alone to go in and out of the soul, to excite motions in it, attracting it entirely to the love of his divine Majesty. I say, without cause. that is, without any previous perception or knowledge of any object from which such consolation might come to the soul, by means of its own acts of the understanding and will.

3. When a cause has preceded, it is possible for the good as well as the bad angel to afford consolation to the soul, but with opposite intentions: the good angel for the advantage of the soul, that it may progress and advance from good to better; the bad angel for the contrary, that he may bring it henceforward to yield to his wicked and malicious designs.

4. It belongs to the bad angel, transfiguring himself into an angel of light, to enter with the devout soul, and to come out his own way; that is to say, to begin by inspiring good and holy thoughts in conformity with the dispositions of the just soul, and afterward gradually to endeavor to gain his end, by drawing the soul into his secret snares and perverse intentions.

5. We ought to be very careful to watch the course of such thoughts; and if the beginning, middle, and end are all good, leading to all that is good, this is a mark of the

good angel; but if the thoughts suggested end in something bad or distracting, or less good than that which the soul had determined to follow, or if they weaken, disturb, or disquiet the soul, taking away the peace, the tranquility, and the quiet she enjoyed before, it is a clear sign that they proceed from the bad spirit, the enemy of our advancement and of our eternal salvation.

6. When the enemy of our human nature has been discovered and recognized by his serpent's tail and by the bad end to which he leads, it is profitable for him who has been thus tempted by him to examine afterward the course of the good thoughts suggested to him, and their beginning, and to remark how little by little the enemy contrived to make him fall from the state of sweetness and spiritual delight he was in, until he brought him to his own depraved purpose; that by the experience and knowledge thus acquired and noted he may be on his guard for the future against his accustomed deceits.

7. In the case of those who are making progress from good to better, the good angel touches the soul gently, lightly, and sweetly, as a drop of water entering into a sponge; and the evil spirit touches it sharply, and with noise and disturbance, like a drop of water falling on a rock. In the case of those

who go from bad to worse, spirits touch it in the contrary manner: and the reason of this difference is the disposition of the soul, according as it is contrary or similar to these angels; for when it is contrary to them they enter with perceptible commotion and disturbance; but when it is similar to them, they enter in silence, as into their own house, through the open doors.

8. When there is consolation without any preceding cause—tho there be no deceit in it, inasmuch as it proceeds only from God our Lord, as before explained—nevertheless the spiritual person to whom God gives this consolation ought with great watchfulness and care to examine and to distinguish the exact period of the actual consolation from the period which follows it, in which the soul continues fervent and feels the remains of the divine favor and consolation lately received; for in this second period it often happens that by its own thoughts, from its own habits, and in consequence of its conceptions and judgments, whether by the suggestion of the good or the evil spirit, it makes various resolves and plans, which are not inspired immediately by God our Lord; and hence it is necessary that they be thoroughly well examined before they receive entire credit and are carried out into effect.

An Invocation of Henry Ward Beecher

We send our voices and our thanksgiving forth to thee, not as to one afar off, to whom our songs become faint from the distance; for thou art a God near unto every one of us. And not alone dost thou hear that which we speak: that which we think sounds in thine ear; and that which we feel and that which lies fallow both of thought and feeling are perfectly well known unto thee. Accept not only our thought and feeling, but all those unmeasured elements from which spring both thought and feeling. And grant to us, to-day, that divine pressure, that molding power, by which all our inward life is shaped which issues forth in conduct. Consecrate us, and make us sons of God, so that our innermost and spontaneous outcry toward thee shall be, evermore, Father. Bless us in reading, in singing, in speaking, in every service of song, at our homes, in our thoughts, in our labor, in all the schools where we may be placed, and make it a day of heaven to us.

SELECTIONS FROM
The Benefit of Christ's Death

BY

AONIO PALEARIO

AONIO PALEARIO

Italian humanist and martyr; born at Veroli about 1500; burned at the stake at Rome July 3, 1570. He studied in Rome in 1520 and after. He was teacher at the university at Sienna in 1530, and published a didactic poem, "De immortalitate animarun" (Lyons, 1536). About 1540 a reaction occurred in his religious views, and in 1542, charges of heresy were grounded on his tract on "The Benefit of Christ's Death." In 1546 he obtained a professorship at Lucca. It may have been here that he completed a second polemic against Rome: "Actio in pontifices Romanos et eorum asseclas" (Amsterdam, 1696; Jena, 1728). Threatened at Lucca by the readiness of the Senate to gratify the demands of the Curia, he withdrew in 1555, finding a position at Milan. Altho again accused by the Inquisition (1559), he vindicated himself in a tract, "Pro se ipso," and was acquitted. A third time (1567) he was subject to persecution, the points of accusation being that he had taught justification by faith, denied the doctrine of purgatory, disparaged monasticism, and censured the practise of burying the dead within the churches. He suffered much hardship and languished in prison, but held fast to his convictions.

In What Wise the Christian Is Clothed With Jesus Christ

Altho that by the things aforesaid[1] a man may easily and plainly enough perceive how a Christian may clothe himself with Jesus Christ, yet, nevertheless, I mind to speak a little of it, assuring myself that unto the good and faithful Christian it can seem neither grievous nor troublesome to speak thereof, altho the thing were repeated a thousand times. Therefore I say that the Christian knoweth that Jesus Christ, together with all his righteousness, holiness, and innocency, is his own through faith. And, like as when a man purposeth to present himself before some great lord or prince, he laboreth to array himself in some fair and costly apparel; even so, when the Christian is decked and arrayed with the innocency of Christ and with all his perfec-

---

[1] The preceding chapters are on the following subjects: Original Sin, and Man's Wretchedness; How the Law was given by God, to the End that we, Knowing our Sin, and having not any Hope of Ability to make Ourselves Righteous by our own Works, should have Recourse to God's Mercy, and unto the Righteousness of Faith; How the Forgiveness of our Sins, our Justification, and our Salvation, depend upon Jesus Christ; Of the Effects of Lively Faith, and of the Union of Man's Soul with Jesus Christ.

tion, he presenteth himself boldly before God
the Lord of all, assuring himself that, through
Christ's merits, he is in as good case as if he
had purchased all that which Jesus Christ
hath purchased and deserved. And, truly,
faith maketh every one of us to possess Christ,
and all that is his, as we possess our own garment.

And, therefore, to be clothed with Jesus
Christ is nothing else but to believe for a
certainty that Christ is wholly ours; and so
is he, in very deed, if we believe so, and hold
ourselves assured that by the same heavenly
garment we be received into favor before God.
For it is most certain that he, as a most dear
Father, hath given us his Son, meaning that
all his righteousness, and all that ever he is,
can do, or hath done, should be in our power
and jurisdiction, in such wise as it should be
lawful for us to make our boast of them, as if
we had done, purchased, and deserved them
by our own strength. And whosoever believeth this shall find that his belief is good
and true, as we have showed heretofore. Then
must the Christian have a stedfast faith and
belief, that all the goods, all the graces, and
all the riches of Jesus Christ are his; for,
sith that God hath given us Jesus Christ himself, how should it be possible that he hath
not given us all things with him? Now, if

this be true, as true it is indeed, the Christian may rightly say, I am the child of God; and Jesus Christ is my brother. I am lord of heaven and earth, and of hell and of death, and of the law; insomuch as the law can not accuse me, nor lay any curse upon me, because the righteousness of God is become mine. And this faith is it alone that maketh a man to be called a Christian, and which clotheth him with Jesus Christ; as we have said afore. And boldly may this be called a great mystery whereunder are contained marvelous things, and things not heard of, concerning that great God, which can not enter into man's heart except God do first soften it with his holy grace; as he hath promised to do by his holy prophet, saying, "I will give you a new heart, and I will put a new mind into you, and I will take away the stony heart out of your body, and I will give you a heart of flesh."

Now, then, he that believeth not after the said manner that Jesus Christ, with all the goods that he possesseth, is his, can not call himself a true Christian, nor ever have a quiet and joyful conscience, nor a good and fervent courage to do good, but shall easily faint in doing of good works; yea, and moreover he shall never be able to do good works that are truly good. This only belief and trust that we have in the merits of Jesus Christ maketh men true Christians, stout, cheerful, merry, lovers of God, ready to do good works, possessors of God's kingdom and of God himself, and his right dear beloved children, in whom the Holy Ghost doth truly dwell. What heart is so cowardly, cold, and vile, which, considering the inestimable greatness of the gift that God hath bestowed upon him, in giving him his own so well-beloved Son with all his perfectness, is not inflamed with an exceeding earnest desire to become like unto him in good works? specially seeing that the Father hath given him unto us for an example whereon we must continually look, framing our life after such a sort as it may be a true counterpart of the life of Jesus Christ; forasmuch as Christ, as saith St. Peter, "hath suffered for us, leaving us an example, to the end that we should follow his footsteps."

Out of this consideration issueth another kind of clothing of a man's self with Christ, which we may term an example-clothing; forsomuch as the Christian must frame his whole life after the example of Christ, fashioning himself like unto him in all his deeds, words, and thoughts, leaving his former wicked life, and decking himself with the new life, that is to wit, with the life of Christ. By reason whereof St. Paul saith, "Let us cast away the

works of darkness, and put on the armor of
light; not in feasting, nor in drunkenness, nor
in chambering and wantonness, nor in strife;
but put upon you the Lord Jesus Christ, and
make no preparation for the flesh, nor for the
lusts thereof.'' Hereupon the true Christian,
being in love with Jesus Christ, saith in himself: Since Jesus Christ, not having any need
of me, hath redeemed me with his own blood,
and is become poor to enrich me; I will likewise give my good, yea, and my very life, for
the love and welfare of my neighbor. And,
like as I am clothed with Jesus Christ, for
the love he hath borne to me, so will I have
my neighbor in Christ to clothe himself with
me, and with my goods likewise, for the love
that I bear him for Christ's sake. He that
doth not so is no true Christian, for he can
not say that he loveth Jesus Christ, if he love
not the members and brothers of him. And if
we love not our neighbor, for whose sake
Christ hath shed his blood, we can not truly
say that we love Jesus Christ; who, being
equal with God, was obedient to his Father,
even to the death of the cross, and hath loved
and redeemed us, giving himself unto us, with
all that ever he hath. After the same manner,
we, being rich and having abundance of good
things at Christ's hand, must also be obedient
unto God, to offer and give our works and all

that we have, yea, and even ourselves, to our
neighbors and brethren in Jesus Christ, serving them and helping them at their need, and
being to them as another Christ. And, like
as Jesus Christ was lowly and gentle, and far
from all debate and strife, so must we set our
whole mind upon lowliness and meekness, es-
chewing all strife and impatience, as well
which consist in words and reasoning as in
deeds. And, as Jesus Christ hath endured all
the persecutions and spites of the world for
the glory of God, so must we with all patient-
ness cheerfully bear the persecutions and reproaches that are done by false Christians
to all such as will live faithfully in Jesus
Christ; who gave his life for his enemies, and
prayed for them upon the cross; and so must
we also pray always for our enemies, and
willingly spend our life for their welfare.

And this is to follow Christ's steps, according as St. Peter saith. For, when we know
Jesus Christ, with all his riches, to be our
own good (which thing is to be clothed with
Christ and to become pure and clean without
spot), there remaineth nothing more for us to
do, but to glorify God by following the life of
Jesus Christ, and to do to our brethren as
Christ hath done to us; and specially forsomuch as we be warranted by his word, that,
whatsoever we do to his brethren and ours, he

accepteth it as a benefit done to himself. And doubtless, seeing that the true Christians are members of Christ, we can not do either good or evil to the true Christians, but we do it likewise unto Christ; insomuch that he rejoiceth or suffereth in his members. Therefore, like as Jesus Christ is our clothing by faith, so also must we through love become the clothing of our brethren, and have as good care of them as of our own bodies; for they be members of our body, whereof Christ is the head.

And this is the godly love and charity which springeth and proceedeth of the true unfeigned faith, which God hath breathed into his elect; which faith, as saith St. Paul, "worketh by love." Howbeit, forasmuch as the life of our Lord Jesus Christ, wherewithal we must be clothed, was a continual cross, full of troubles, reproaches, and persecutions; if we will fashion ourselves like unto his life, we must continually bear the cross; as he himself saith, "If any man will come after me, let him forsake himself, and take up his cross and follow me."

But the chief cause of this cross is, for that our God purposeth to mortify the affections of our mind and the lusts of our flesh by that exercise; to the end we may conceive in ourselves the great perfection wherein we be com-

prised by our Lord Jesus Christ, by being
grafted into him. Also his will is, that our
faith, being fined like gold in the furnace of
troubles, should shine bright to his glory.
Moreover, his intent is that we, by our infirmities should set out his great power which the
world, in despite of it, beholdeth in us; inasmuch as our frailty becometh strong by
troubles and persecutions, and the more that
it was beaten down and opprest, so much
the more it is strong and stedfast. Whereof
the Apostle Paul saith, "We carry this treasure in earthen vessels, that the excellency
of the power might be God's and not ours. On
all sides we suffer tribulation, but we are not
overcome; we be poor, but not overcome of
poverty; we suffer persecution, but yet are we
not forsaken; we be despised, but yet we
perish not: and so we daily bear about us
the dying of our Lord Jesus Christ in our
body, that the life of Jesus Christ may also be openly showed in us." And, seeing
the case is so, that our Lord Jesus Christ
and all his dear disciples glorified God by
tribulations, let us also embrace them joyfully, and say with the Apostle Paul, "God
forbid that I should glory, save in the cross
of our Lord Jesus Christ"; and let us so deal,
as the world may (whether it will or no) perceive and see with its eyes the wonderful ef-

fects that God worketh in such as sincerely embrace the grace of his gospel. Let us so deal, I say, as the worldlings may see with how great quietness of mind the true Christians endure the loss of their goods, the death of their children, slanders, the diseases of the body, and the persecutions of false Christians; and also that they may see how the only true Christians do worship God in spirit and truth, taking in good worth at his hand whatsoever happeneth, and holding all that he doth to be good, righteous, and holy, praising him always for the same, whether it be in prosperity or adversity, thanking him as a most gracious and loving Father, and acknowledging it for a right great gift of God's goodness to suffer any adversity, and chiefly for the gospel and for following the steps of Christ; especially forasmuch as we know that "tribulation engendereth patience, and patience trial, and trial hope, and hope maketh us not ashamed." I say, that patience engendereth trial; because that, whereas God hath promised help in trouble to such as trust in him, we find it by experience, in that we continue strong and stedfast all the while, and are upholden by the hand of God; which thing we could not do with all the powers that we have of our own. So, then, by patience we find that our Lord giveth us the help that he hath promised us at our need, whereby our hope is confirmed. And it were an over-great unthankfulness, not to trust to such an aid and favor for the time to come, as we have found by experience to be so certain and stedfast heretofore. But what need we so many words? It ought to suffice us to know that the true Christians are through tribulation clothed with the image of our Lord Jesus Christ crucified; which if we bear willingly and with a good heart, we shall in the end be clothed with the image of Jesus Christ glorified. "For, as the passions of Jesus Christ do abound, so through him shall the consolations over-abound; and, if we suffer with him here below for a time, we shall also reign with him there above forever.

A Prayer from the King's Chapel (Boston) Liturgy

We pray thee to compassionate our weakness, O Lord, to guard us in peril, to direct us in doubt, and to save us from falling into sin. From the evil that is around and within us graciously deliver us. Make the path of duty plain before us, and keep us in it even unto the end. AMEN.

Prayers for Several Occasions

BY

JOHN CALVIN

From the Translation

BY

HENRY BEVERIDGE

JOHN CALVIN

Swiss reformer; born at Noyon, Picardy, July 10, 1509; died in Geneva, Switzerland, May 27, 1564. In 1523 he went to Paris to prepare for the priesthood at the Collège de la Marche and the Collège de Montaigu. In 1527 he was given the curacy (nominal) of St. Martin de Martheville. In 1528 his father ordered him to change his studies to law. He left Paris for the university at Orléans, and after that he went to Bourges, where he came under the influence of Melchior Wolmar, a distinguished humanist favorable to the Reformation. While at Bourges he began to preach the reform doctrine. When his father died in 1531 he left Bourges and returned to Paris for study of classics and Hebrew. In Paris, the center of the "new learning" under the teaching of Lefevre and Farel, the excitement became so intense that Calvin was obliged to flee, and went to Basel, where he issued his "Institutes of the Christian Religion" in March, 1536. He arrived in Geneva in July, 1536, where Farel urged him to remain for the work of reformation. In 1538 both Calvin and Farel were expelled. Calvin retreated to Strassburg and devoted himself to theological study. The Genevans, however, invited him back, and in 1541 he returned to Geneva, and took up the task of ordering her affairs according to his high standards. "There he was the founder of a new church polity, which did more than all other influences together to consolidate the scattered forces of the Reformation. By many the system which he founded is regarded as a re-assertion of Augustinianism." Among Calvin's most important works are: "Christianæ Religionis Institutio" (1536); "De Necessitate Reformandæ Ecclesiæ" (1544); and commentaries on the New Testament, Psalms and Genesis.

John Calvin

For the Morning

My God, my Father and Preserver, who of thy goodness has watched over me during the past night and brought me to this day, grant also that I may spend it wholly in the worship and service of thy most holy deity. Let me not think or do or say a single thing which tends not to thy service and submission to thy will, that thus all my actions may aim at thy glory and the salvation of my brethren, while they are taught by my example to serve thee. And as thou art giving light to this world for the purposes of external life by the rays of the sun, so enlighten my mind by the effulgence of thy Spirit, that he may guide me in the way of thy righteousness. To whatever purpose I apply my mind, may the end which I ever propose to myself be thy honor and service. May I expect all happiness from thy grace and goodness only. Let me not attempt anything whatever that is not pleasing to thee.

Grant also, that while I labor for the maintenance of this life and care for the things which pertain to food and raiment, I may raise my mind above them to the blessed and heavenly life which thou hast promised to thy children. Be pleased also, in manifesting thyself to me as the protector of my soul as well as my body, to strengthen and fortify me against all the assaults of the devil, and deliver me from all the dangers which continually beset us in this life. But seeing it is a small thing to have begun unless I also persevere, I therefore entreat thee, O Lord, not only to be my Guide and Director for this day, but to keep me under thy protection to the very end of life, that thus my whole course may be performed under thy superintendence. As I ought to make progress, do thou add daily more and more to the gifts of thy grace until I wholly adhere to thy Son, Jesus Christ, whom we justly regard as the true Son, shining constantly in our minds. In order to my obtaining of thee these great and manifold blessings, forget and out of thy infinite mercy forgive my offenses, as thou hast promised that thou wilt do to those who call upon thee in sincerity.

Grant that I may hear thy voice in the morning, since I have hoped in thee. Show me the way in which I should walk, since I have lifted up my soul unto thee. Deliver me from my enemies, O Lord, I have fled unto thee. Teach me to do thy will, for thou art my God. Let thy good Spirit conduct me to the land of uprightness (Ps. 143:8).

John Calvin

On Preparing to Go to School

[Wherein shall a young man establish his way? If he wisely conduct himself according to thy word. With my heart have I sought thee, allow me not to err from thy precepts.—Ps. 119 : 9. The secret of the Lord is with them that fear him ; and he will make known his covenant unto them.—Ps. 25 : 14.]

O Lord, who art the fountain of all wisdom and learning, since thou of thy special goodness hast granted that my youth is instructed in good arts which may assist me to honest and holy living, grant also by enlightening my mind, which otherwise labors under blindness, that I may be fit to acquire knowledge ; strengthen my memory faithfully to retain what I may have learned ; and govern my heart, that I may be willing and even eager to profit, lest the opportunity which thou now givest me be lost through my sluggishness. Be pleased therefore to infuse thy Spirit into me, the Spirit of understanding, of truth, judgment, and prudence, lest my study be without success, and the labor of my teacher be in vain.

In whatever kind of study I engage, enable me to remember to keep its proper end in view, namely to know thee in Christ Jesus thy Son ; and may every thing that I learn assist me to observe the right rule of godliness. And seeing thou promisest that thou wilt bestow wisdom on babes and such as are humble, and the knowledge of thyself on the upright in heart, while thou declarest that thou wilt cast down the wicked and the proud, so that they will fade away in their ways, I entreat that thou wouldst be pleased to turn me to true humility, that thus I may show myself teachable and obedient first of all to thyself, and then to those also who by thy authority are placed over me. Be pleased at the same time to root out all vicious desires from my heart, and inspire it with an earnest desire of seeking thee. Finally, let the only end at which I aim be so to qualify myself in early life, that when I grow up I may serve thee in whatever station thou mayest assign me. AMEN.

Blessing At Table

[All look unto thee, O Lord; and thou givest them their meat in due season; that thou givest them they gather; thou openest thine hand, and they are filled with all things in abundance.—Ps. 104:27. Man liveth not by bread alone, but by every word which proceedeth from the mouth of God.—Deut. 8:3.]

O Lord, in whom is the source and inexhaustible fountain of all good things, pour out thy blessing upon us, and sanctify to our use the meat and drink which are the gifts of thy kindness toward us, that we, using them soberly and frugally as thou enjoinest, may eat with a pure conscience. Grant, also, that we may always both with true heartfelt gratitude acknowledge, and with our lips proclaim thee our Father and the Giver of all good, and while enjoying bodily nourishment, aspire with special longing of heart after the bread of thy doctrine, by which our souls may be nourished in the hope of eternal life, through Christ Jesus our Lord. AMEN.

Thanksgiving After Meat

[Let all nations praise the Lord: let all the people sing praises to God.—Ps. 117:1.]

We give thanks, O God and Father, for the many mercies which thou of thy infinite goodness art constantly bestowing upon us; both in that by supplying all the helps which we need to sustain the present life, thou showest that thou hast a care even of our bodies, and more especially in that thou hast deigned to beget us again to the hope of the better life which thou hast revealed to us by thy holy gospel. And we beseech thee not to allow our minds to be chained down to earthly thoughts and cares, as if they were buried in our bodies. Rather cause that we may stand with eyes upraised in expectation of thy Son Jesus Christ, till he appear from heaven for our redemption and salvation. AMEN.

Prayer at Night on Going to Sleep

O Lord God, who hast given man the night
for rest, as thou hast created the day in which
he may employ himself in labor, grant, I pray,
that my body may so rest during this night
that my mind cease not to be awake to thee,
nor my heart faint or be overcome with torpor,
preventing it from adhering stedfastly to
the love of thee. While laying aside my cares
to relax and relieve my mind, may I not, in
the meanwhile, forget thee, nor may the re-
membrance of thy goodness and grace, which
ought always to be deeply engraven on my
mind, escape my memory. In like manner,
also, as the body rests may my conscience
enjoy rest. . . . Be pleased to keep me so
chaste and unpolluted, not less in mind than
in body, and safe from all dangers, that my
sleep itself may turn to the glory of thy name.
But since this day has not passed away without my having in many ways offended thee
through my proneness to evil, in like manner
as all things are now covered by the darkness
of night, so let everything that is sinful in
me lie buried in thy mercy. Hear me, O God,
Father and Preserver, through Jesus Christ
thy Son. AMEN.

A Declaration of the True Nature and Object of Prayer

BY

JOHN KNOX

JOHN KNOX

The place of birth of the great Scottish reformer and minister of St. Giles, Edinburgh, was probably Giffordgate, a suburb of Haddington. The date of his birth is uncertain; he died at Edinburgh, November 24, 1572. He attended the grammar school at Haddington and then he went either to the University of Glasgow, where the name of "John Knox" occurs among the *incorporati* in 1522, or to St. Andrews, where he is stated by Beza to have studied under the celebrated John Major. He was ordained to the priesthood at some date prior to 1540 and his change to the Protestant faith came about the end of 1545, under the influence of George Wishart, the reformer. Knox was called to the Protestant ministry of St. Andrews. In 1547 St. Andrews yielded to the French fleet, and Knox was thrown into the galleys on the Loire, where he spent nineteen months of hardship as a galley slave. He was released in 1549. He served for five years as a minister of the English Church; and in 1551 he was appointed a royal chaplain. After the death of Edward VI. he traveled on the Continent, and in 1554 accepted a call to the English church at Frankfort, and in July, 1556, to Geneva. He returned to his native land May 2, 1559, and became the leader of the Reformers. "The doctrine, worship, and government of the Roman Church were overthrown by the Parliament of 1560, and Protestantism was established as the national religion. Knox, assisted by five other ministers, formulated the Confession of Faith adopted at this time and drew up the constitution of the new church." The works of Knox are best consulted in the edition by David Laing (6 vols., Edinburgh, 1864), which includes the principal sources for a biography, namely his "History of the Reformation," his "Correspondence," and other historical matter.

Unto the Small and Dispersed Flock of Jesus Christ

How necessary is the right invocation of God's name (otherwise called perfect prayer) becometh no Christian to misknaw,[1] seeing it is the very branch which springeth forth of true faith, whereof if any man be destitute, notwithstanding he be endowed with whatsoever other virtues, yet in the presence of God is he reputed for no Christian at all. Therefore a manifest sign it is, that such as in prayer always are negligent do understand nothing of perfect faith. For if the fire be without heat, or the burning lamp without light, then true faith may be without fervent prayer. But because, in times past was (and yet alas! with no small number is) that raconit[2] to be prayer which in the sight of God was and is nothing less, I intend shortly (briefly) to touch the circumstances thereof.

WHAT PRAYER IS: Who will pray, must know and understand that prayer is an earnest and familiar talking with God, to whom we declare our miseries, whose support and help we implore and desire in our adversities,

---

[1] To be ignorant or mistaken.   [2] Reckoned.

157

and whom we laud and praise for our benefits received. So that prayer containeth the exposition of our dolouris,[3] the desire of God's defense, and the praising of this magnificent name, as the Psalms of David clearly do teach.

WHAT IS TO BE OBSERVED IN PRAYER: That this be most reverently done, should provoke us the consideration in whose presence we stand, to whom we speak, and what we desire; standing in the presence of the omnipotent Creator of heaven and earth, and of all the contents thereof; to whom assist and serve a thousand thousand of angels, giving obedience to his eternal majesty; and speaking unto him who knoweth the secrets of our hearts, before whom dissimulation and lies are always odious and hateful, and asking that thing which may be most to his glory and to the comfort of our conscience. But diligently should we attend, that such things as may offend his godly presence, to the uttermost of our power, may be removed. And first, that worldly cares and fleshly cogitations (such as draw us from contemplation of our God) be expelled from us, that we may freely without interruption call upon God. But, how difficult and hard is this one thing in prayer to perform knoweth none better than such as in their prayers are not content to

[3] Troubles, sorrows.

remain within the bounds of their own vanity, but, as it were ravished, do intend[4] to a purity allowed of God; asking not such things as the foolish reason of man desireth, but which may be pleasant and acceptable in God's presence. Our adversary, Satan, at all times compassing us about, is never more busy than when we address and bend ourselves to prayer. O! how secretly and subtly creepeth he into our breasts, and, calling us back from God, causeth us to forget what we have to do; so that frequently when we (with all reverence) should speak to God, we find our hearts talking with the vanities of the world, or with the foolish imaginations of our own conceit.

How THE SPIRIT MAKETH INTERCESSION FOR Us: So that without the Spirit of God supporting our infirmities (mightily making intercession for us with incessibill[5] groans, which can not be exprest with tongue), there is no hope that anything we can desire according to God's will. I mean not that the holy God doth mourn or pray, but that he stirreth up our minds, giving unto us a desire or boldness for to pray, and causeth us to mourn when we are extracted or pulled therefrom. Which things to conceive no strength of man sufficeth, neither is able of itself; but hereof it is plain, that such as

---

[4] Do strive to attain.   [5] Unceasing.

understand not what they pray, or expound not, or declare not the desire of their hearts clearly in God's presence, and in time of prayer (to their possibility) do not expel vain cogitations from their minds, profit nothing in prayer.

WHY WE SHOULD PRAY, AND ALSO UNDERSTAND WHAT WE DO PRAY: But men will object and say, Albeit we understand not what we pray, yet God understandeth, who knoweth the secrets of our hearts; he knoweth also what we need, altho we expone (set forth) not, or declare not, our necessities unto him. Such men verily declare themselves never to have understanding what perfect prayer meant, nor to what end Jesus Christ commandeth us to pray; which is, first, that our hearts may be inflamed with continual fear, honor, and love of God, to whom we run for support and help whensoever danger or necessity requireth; that we so learning to notify our desires in his presence, he may teach us what is to be desired and what not. Secondly, that we, knowing our petitions to be granted by God alone, to him only we must render and give laud and praise, and that we ever having his infinite goodness fixt in our minds, may constantly abide to receive that which with fervent prayer we desire.

WHY GOD DEFERRETH TO GRANT OUR

PRAYERS: For some time God deferreth or prolongeth to grant our petitions for the exercise and trial of our faith, and not that he sleepeth or is absent from us at any time, but that with more gladness we might receive that which with long expectation we have abidden; that thereby we, assured of his eternal providence (so far as the infirmity of our corrupt and most weak nature will permit), doubt not but his merciful hand shall relieve us in most urgent necessity and extreme tribulation. Therefore, such men as teach us that necessarily it is not required that we understand what we pray, because God knoweth what we need, would also teach us that neither we honor God, nor yet refer or give unto him thanks for benefits received; for how shall we honor and praise him whose goodness and liberality we know not? And how shall we know unless we receive and some time have experience? And how shall we know that we have received unless we know verily what we have asked?

The second thing to be observed in perfect prayer is that, standing in the presence of God, we be found such as do bear to his holy law reverence, earnestly repenting our iniquity past and intending to lead a new life; for otherwise in vain are all our prayers, as it is written, "Whoso withdraweth his ear that he may not hear the law, his prayer shall be abominable" (Prov. 8). Likewise Isaiah and Jeremiah say thus, "You shall multiply your prayers, and I shall not hear, because your hands are full of blood," that is, of all cruelty and mischievous works. Also the spirit of God appeareth by the mouth of the blind (whom Jesus Christ did illuminate) by these words, "We know that God heareth not sinners" (John 9), that is, such as glory and do continue in iniquity; so that of necessity, true repentance must needs be had, and go before perfect prayer or sincere invocation of God's name.

WHEN SINNERS ARE NOT HEARD OF GOD: And unto these two precedents must be annexed the third, which is, the dejection of ourselves in God's presence, utterly refusing and casting of our own justice, with all cogitations and opinion thereof. And let us not think that we should be heard for anything proceeding of ourselves, for all such as advance, boast, or depend anything upon their own justice, from the presence of his mercy, repelleth and holdeth with the high proud Pharisee: and therefore, the most holy men we find in prayers most dejected and humbled. David saith, "O Lord, our Savior, help us, be merciful unto our sins for thy own sake. Remember not our old iniquities. But haste thou, O Lord, and let thy mercy prevent us'' (Ps. 79). Jeremiah saith, ''If our iniquities bear testimony against us, do thou according to thy own name''; and behold Isaiah, ''Thou art angry,[6] O Lord, because we have sinned and are replenished with all wickedness; and our justice is like a defiled cloth. But now, O Lord, thou art our Father; we are clay, thou art the workman, and we are the workmanship of thy hands; be not angry,[7] O Lord, remember not our iniquities forever'' (Isa. 64). And Daniel, greatly commended of God maketh in his prayer most humble confession in these words, ''We be sinners, and have offended; we have done ungodly, and fallen from thy commandment, therefore, not in our own righteousness make we our prayers before thee, but thy most right and great mercies bring we forth for us. O Lord, hear! O Lord, be merciful and spare us! O Lord, attend, help, and cease not; my God, even for thy own name's sake do it; for thy city and thy people are called after thy own name'' (Dan. 9). Behold that in these prayers is no mention of their own justice, their own satisfaction, or their own merits. But most humble confession, proceeding from a sorrow-

---

[6] In the edition of 1554, ''Thou art crabbed.''
[7] *Ib.* ''Be not crabbed.''

ful and penitent heart; having nothing whereupon it might depend, but the free mercy of
God alone, who had promised to be their God
(that is, their help, comfort, defender, and
deliverer), as he hath also done to us by Jesus
Christ in time of tribulation; and that they
despair not, but after the acknowledging of
their sins, called for mercy and obtained the
same. Wherefore it is plain, that such men
as, in their prayers, have respect to any virtue
proceeding of themselves, thinking thereby
their prayers to be accepted, never prayed
aright.

WHAT FASTING AND ALMS-DEEDS ARE WITH[8]
PRAYER: And albeit to fervent prayer be
joined fasting, watching, and alms-deeds, yet
are none of them the cause that God doth
accept our prayers; but they are spurs which
suffer us not to vary, but make us more able
to continue in prayer, which the mercy of
God doth accept. But here it may be objected, that David prayeth, "Keep my life,
O Lord, for I am holy; O Lord, save my
soul, for I am innocent; and suffer me not
to be consumed" (comp. Ps. 33 and 86). Also
Hezekiah, "Remember, Lord, I beseech thee,
that I have walked righteously before thee,
and that I have wrought that which is good
in thy sight" (2 Kings 20:3). These words

[8] In the edition of 1554, "Without."

are not spoken of men glorious, neither yet trusting in their own works. But herein they testify themselves to be the sons of God by regeneration; to whom he promised always to be merciful, and at all times to hear their prayers.

THE CAUSE OF THEIR BOLDNESS WAS JESUS CHRIST: And so their words sprung from a wonted, constant, and fervent faith, surely believing that as God of his infinite mercy had called them to his knowledge, not suffering them to walk after their own natural wickedness, but partly had taught them to conform them to his holy law; and that for the promised Seed's sake; so might he not leave them destitute of comfort, consolation, and defense in so great and extreme necessity. And so their justice allege they, not to glory thereof or to put trust therein, but to strengthen and confirm them in God's promises. And this consolation I would wish all Christians in their prayers: a testimony of a good conscience to assure them of God's promises; but to obtain what they ask must only depend upon him, all opinion and thought of our own justice laid aside. And, moreover, David, in the words above, compareth himself with King Saul and with the rest of his enemies, who wrongfully did persecute him; desiring of God that they prevail not against him, as he would say, Unjustly do they persecute me, and therefore according to my innocence defend me. For otherwise he confesseth himself most grievously to have offended God, as in the precedent places he clearly testifieth.

HYPOCRISY IS NOT ALLOWED WITH GOD: Thirdly, in prayer is to be observed, that what we ask of God, that we must earnestly desire the same, acknowledging us to be indigent and void thereof; and that God alone may grant the petition of our hearts, when his good will and pleasure is. For nothing is more odious before God than hypocrisy and dissimulation, that is, when men do ask of God things whereof they have no need, or that they believe to obtain by others than God alone. As if a man ask of God remission of his sins, thinking never the less to obtain the same by his own works, or by other men's merits, doth mock with God and deceive himself. And in such cases do a great number offend, principally the mighty and rich of the earth, who for a common custom will pray this part of the Lord's Prayer, "Give us this day our daily bread," that is, a moderate and reasonable sustentation; and yet their own hearts will testify that they need not so to pray, seeing they abound in all worldly solace and felicity. I mean not that rich men should not pray this part of prayer, but I would they understood what they ought to pray in it (whereof I intend after to speak), and that they ask nothing whereof they felt not themselves marvelous indigent and needful. For unless we call in verity, we shall not grant; and except we speak with our whole heart, we shall not find him.

The fourth rule necessary to be followed in prayer is, A sure hope to obtain what we ask. For nothing more offendeth God than when we ask doubting whether he will grant our petitions; for in so doing we doubt if God be true, if he be mighty and good; such (saith James) obtain nothing of God. And therefore Jesus Christ commandeth that we firmly believe to obtain whatsoever we ask; for all things is possible unto him that believeth. And therefore, in our prayers always is to be expelled desperation. I mean not that any man in extremity of trouble can be without a present dolor, and without a greater fear of trouble to follow.

TROUBLES ARE THE SPURS TO STIR US TO PRAY: Trouble and fear are very spurs to prayer; for when man, compassed about with vehement calamities and vexed with continual solicitude, having by help of man no hope for deliverance, with sore opprest and punished heart fearing also greater punishment to follow, from the deep pit of tribulation doth call to God for comfort and support; such prayer ascendeth into God's presence and returneth not in vain.

GOD DELIVERETH HIS OWN FROM THEIR TROUBLE AND ENEMIES: As David, in the vehement persecution of Saul, hunted and chased from every hold, fearing that one day or other he should fall into the hands of his persecutors, after he had complained that no place of rest was left for him, vehemently prayed, saying, "O Lord, which art my God, in whom I only trust, save me from them that persecute me, and deliver me from my enemies. Let not this man (meaning Saul) devour my life, as a lion doth his prey: for of none seek I comfort but of thee alone."

In the midst of these anguishes the goodness of God sustained him, that the present tribulation was tolerable, and the infallible promises of God so assured him of deliverance that fear was partly mitigated and gone, as plainly appeareth to such as diligently marketh the process of his prayers. For after long menacing and threatening made to him of his enemy, he concludeth with these words, "The dolor which he intended for me shall fall upon his own pate; and the violence wherewith he would have opprest me shall cast down his own head.

But I will magnify the Lord according to his justice, and shall praise the name of the Most Highest.'' This is not written for David only, but for all such as shall suffer tribulation to the end of the world. For I, the writer hereof (let this be said to the laud and praise of God alone), in anguish of mind and vehement tribulation and affliction, called to the Lord when not only the ungodly, but even my faithful brethren, yea, and my own self, that is all natural understanding, judged my cause[9] to be irremediable. And yet in my greatest calamity, and when my pains were most cruel, would his eternal wisdom that my hands should write far contrary to the judgment of carnal reason, which his mercy hath proved true. Blessed be his holy name! And therefore dare I be bold, in the verity of God's word, to promise that notwithstanding the vehemency of trouble, the long continuance thereof, the desperation of all men, the fearfulness, danger, dolor, and anguish of our own hearts, yet if we call constantly to God, beyond expectation of all men he shall deliver.

WHERE CONSTANT PRAYER IS, THERE THE PETITION IS GRANTED: Let no man think himself unworthy to call and pray to God

[9] Knox here refers to his bodily and mental sufferings during the time of his confinement on board the French galley.

because he hath grievously offended his
majesty in times past; but let him bring to
God a sorrowful and repenting heart, saying
with David, "Heal my soul, O Lord, for I
have offended against thee. Before I was
afflicted, I transgressed, but now let me observe thy commandments." To mitigate or
ease the sorrows of our wounded conscience
two plasters hath our most prudent Physician
provided to give us encouragement to pray
(notwithstanding the knowledge of offenses
committed), that is, a precept and a promise.
The precept or commandment to pray is
universal, frequently inculcated and repeated
in God's Scriptures: "Ask, and it shall be
given unto you" (Matt. 7); "Call upon me
in the day of trouble" (Ps. 40); "Watch
and pray that ye fall not into temptation"
(Matt. 26); "I command that ye pray ever
without ceasing" (Tim. 2); "Make depreca-
tions incessible (unceasing), and give thanks
in all things" (1 Thess. 5). Which commandments whoso contemneth or despiseth
doth equally sin with him that doth steal;
for in this commandment "thou shalt not
steal" is a precept negative; so "thou shalt
pray" is a commandment affirmative. And
God requireth equal obedience of and to all
his commandments. Yet more boldly will I
say, he who, when necessity constraineth, de-

sireth not support and help of God, doth provoke his wrath no less than such as make false gods or openly deny God.

HE THAT PRAYETH NOT IN TROUBLE, DENIETH GOD: For like as it is to know no physician or medicine, or in knowing them refuse to use and receive the same; so not to call upon God in thy tribulation, is like as if thou didst not know God, or else [didst] utterly deny him.

NOT TO PRAY IS A SIN MOST ODIOUS: O! why cease we then to call instantly to his mercy, having his commandment so to do? Above all our iniquities, we work manifest contempt and despising of him when, by negligence, we delay to call for his gracious support. Who doth call upon God obeyeth his will, and findeth therein no small consolation, knowing nothing is more acceptable to his majesty than humble obedience.

To this commandment he addeth his most undoubted promise in many places, "Ask, and ye shall receive; seek, and ye shall find" (Matt. 7). And by the Prophet Jeremiah God saith: "Ye shall call upon me, and I shall hear you. Ye shall seek and shall find me" (Jer. 28). And by Isaiah, he saith: "May the father forget his natural son, or the mother the child of her womb! and altho they do, yet shall I not forget such as call

171

upon me." And hereto correspond and agree the words of Jesus Christ, saying, "If ye being wicked can give good gifts to your children, much more my heavenly Father shall give the Holy Ghost to them that ask him" (Luke 11). And that we should not think God to be absent or not to hear us, accuseth Moses saying, "There is no nation that have their Gods so adherent (present), or near unto them as our God, which is present at all our prayers" (Deut. 4). Also the psalmist, "Near is the Lord unto all that call upon him in verity." And Christ saith, "Wheresoever two or three are gathered together in my name, there am I in the midst of them."

READINESS OF GOD TO HEAR SINNERS: That we shall not think that God will not hear us, Isaiah saith, "Before ye cry I shall hear, and while they speak I shall answer"; and also, "If at even come sorrow or calamity, before the morning spring I shall reduce[10] and bring gladness." And these most comfortable words doth the Lord speak not to carnal Israel only, but to all men sore opprest, abiding God's deliverance: "For a moment and a little season have I turned my face from thee, but in everlasting mercy shall I comfort thee."

[10] To bring back (Lat. *reducere*).

THE HOPE TO OBTAIN OUR PETITIONS
SHOULD DEPEND UPON THE PROMISES OF GOD:
O! hard are the hearts whom so manifold,
most sweet, and sure promises doth not
mollify; whereupon should depend the hope
to obtain our petitions. The indignity or un-
worthiness of ourselves is not to be regarded;
for albeit (altho) to the chosen which
are departed in holiness and purity of life
we be far inferiors, yet in that part we are
equal, in that we have the same commandment
to pray and the same promise to be heard.
For his gracious majesty esteemeth not the
prayer neither granteth the petition for any
dignity of the person that prayeth, but for
his promises's sake only; and therefore saith
David, "Thou hast promised unto thy servant,
O Lord, that thou wilt build a house for him,
wherefore thy servant hath found in his heart
to pray in thy sight, now even so, O Lord,
thou art God, and thy words are true. Thou
hast spoken these things unto thy servant,
begin therefore to do according to thy promise;
multiply, O Lord, the household of thy servant." Behold, David altogether dependeth
upon God's promise. As also did Jacob, who
after he had confest himself unworthy of
all the benefits received, yet durst he ask
greater benefits in time to come, and that because God had promised. In the like manner,

let us be encouraged to ask whatsoever the goodness of God hath freely promised. What we should ask principally, we shall hereafter declare.

OBSERVATION IN GODLY PRAYER: The fifth observation which godly prayer requireth, is perfect knowledge of the Advocate, Intercessor, and Mediator.

OF NECESSITY WE MUST HAVE A MEDIATOR: For, seeing no man is of himself worthy to compare or appear in God's presence, by reason that in all men continually resteth sin, which by itself doth offend the majesty of God; raising all debate, strife, hatred, and division betwixt his inviolable justice and us. For the which, unless satisfaction be made by another than by ourselves, so little hope resteth that anything from him we can attain that no surety with him may we have at all. To exempt us from this horrible confusion our most merciful Father has given unto us his only Son to be unto us justice, wisdom, sanctification, and holiness. If in him we faithfully believe, we are so clad that we may with boldness present ourselves and appear before the throne of God's mercy; doubting nothing but whatsoever we ask by our Mediator, that same we shall obtain most assuredly.

NOTE DILIGENTLY, BY WHOM WE MUST PRAY: Here is most diligently to be observed,

that without our Mediator, Forespeaker, and
Peace-maker we enter not into prayer; for
the incalling of such as pray without Jesus
Christ are not only vain, but also they are
odious and abominable before God. Which
thing to us in the Levitical priesthood most
evidently was prefigured and declared; for as
within the *Sanctum Sanctorum* (that is, the
most Holy Place), entered no man but the
high priest alone: and as all sacrifices offered
by any other than by priests only provoked the
wrath of God upon the sacrifice maker, so who
doth intend to enter into God's presence, or
to make prayers without Jesus Christ, shall
find nothing but fearful judgment and horrible damnation. . . .

WHEN WE BE NOT HEARD: For as the
law is a statute that we shall call upon God,
and as the promise is made that he shall hear
us, so are we commanded only to call by
Jesus Christ, by whom alone our petitions we
obtain; for in him alone are all the promises
of God confirmed and complete; whereof,
without all controversy, it is plain that such
as have called, or calleth presently, unto God
by any other name than by Jesus Christ alone
doth nothing regard God's will, but obstinate-
ly prevaricateth and doth against his commandments. And therefore, obtain not they
their petitions, neither yet have entrance to

his mercy. For no man cometh to the Father
(saith Jesus Christ) but by me. He is the
right way; who declineth from this erreth
and goeth wrong; he is our leader, whom without we follow we shall walk in darkness; and
he alone is our captain, without whom
neither praise nor victory ever shall we obtain.

INTERCESSION TO SAINTS: Against such as
depend upon the intercession of saints no
otherwise will I contend but shortly (briefly),
touch the properties of a perfect Mediator.
First are the words most sure of Paul, "A
mediator is not the mediator of one," that is,
wheresoever is required a mediator there are
also two parties; to wit, one party offendant,
and the other party which is offended; which
parties by themselves may in no wise be
reconciled. Secondly, the mediator which
taketh upon him the reconciling of these two
parties must be such a one as, having trust
and favor of both parties, yet in some things
must differ from both, and must be clear and
innocent also of the crime committed against
the party offended. Let this be more plain
by this subsequent declaration: The eternal
God standing upon the one part, and all
natural men descending of Adam upon the
other part. The infinite justice of God is so
offended with the transgression of all men

John Knox

that in no wise can amity be made, except such one be found as fully may make satisfaction for man's offenses. Among the sons of men none was found able; for all they were found criminal in the fall of one. And God, infinite in justice, must abhor the society and sacrifice of sinners.

ANGELS CAN NOT BE MEDIATORS: And unto the angels what prevailed the prevarication of man, who (albeit they would have interposed themselves mediator) yet had not the justice infinite. Who then shall here be found the Peace-maker? Surely the infinite goodness and mercy of God might not suffer the perpetual loss and repudiation of his creatures; and therefore his eternal wisdom provided such a Mediator, having wherewith to satisfy the justice of God, differing also from the Godhead—his only Son, clad in the nature of manhood, who interposed himself a Mediator, not as man only.

JESUS CHRIST, GOD AND MAN, OUR MEDIATOR: For the pure humanity of Christ (of itself) might neither make intercession nor satisfaction for us, but God and man. In that he is God, he might complete the will of the Father, and in that he is man, pure and clean without spot or sin, he might offer sacrifice for the purgation of our sins and satisfaction of God's justice. So, without saints have these two, Godhead equal with the Father and humanity without sin, the office of mediators saints may not usurp.

But here will be objected, Who knoweth not Jesus Christ to be the only Mediator of our redemption; but that impedeth or letteth (hindereth) nothing saints and holy men to be mediators and to make intercession for us. As tho that Jesus Christ had been but one hour our Mediator, and after had resigned the office unto his servants!

WHO MAKETH OTHER MEDIATORS NOR JESUS CHRIST TAKETH HONOR FROM HIM: Do not such men gentilie[11] entreat Jesus Christ, detracting from him such portion of his honor? Otherwise speaketh the Scriptures of God, testifying him to have been made man, and to have proved our infirmities; to have suffered death willingly; to have overcome the same; and all to this end, that he might be our perpetual High Sovereign Priest, in whose place or dignity none other might enter. As John saith, "If any man sin, we have an advocate with the Father, even Jesus Christ the just" (Heb. chaps 6, 7, 9, 10).

Mark well these words: John saith, We have presently a sufficient advocate, whom Paul affirmeth to sit at the right hand of God the Father, and to be the only Mediator between

[11] Gentilly, that is, respectfully (spoken ironically).

God and men. "For he alone (saith Ambrose) is our mouth, by whom we speak to God; he is our eyes, by whom we see God, and also our right hand, by whom we offer any thing unto the Father"; who, unless he make intercession, neither we, neither any of the saints, may have any society or fellowship with God. What creature may say to God the Father; "Let mankind be received into thy favor for the pain of his transgression that have I sustained in my own body? For his cause was I compassed with all infirmities, and so became the most contemned and despised of all men; and yet in my mouth was found no guile or deceit, but always obedient to thy will, suffering most grievous death for mankind. And, therefore, behold not the sinner but me, who, by my infinite justice,[12] hath perfectly satisfied for his offenses." May any other (Jesus Christ excepted) in these words make intercession for sinners? If they may not, then are they neither mediators nor yet intercessors. "For albeit (saith Augustine) Christians do commend one another unto God in their prayers, yet make they not intercession, neither dare they usurp the office of a mediator; no not Paul, albeit under the Head he was a principal member, because he commendeth himself to the prayers

---

[12] Justice, or righteousness.

of faithful men.'' But if any do object, such is not the condition of the saints departed, who now hath put off mortality, and beareth no longer the fragility of the flesh; which albeit I grant to be most true, yet are they all compelled to cast their crowns before him that doth sit in (on) the throne, acknowledging themselves to have been delivered from great affliction, to have been purged by the blood of the lamb; and therefore none of them do attempt to be a mediator, seeing they neither have being nor justice of themselves.

But in so great light of the gospel which now is beginning (praise be to the Omnipotent!), it is not necessary upon such matter long to remain. Some say, We will use but one mediator, Jesus Christ, to God the Father; but we must have saints, and chiefly the Virgin Mary, the mother of Jesus Christ, to pray for us unto him.

AGAINST SUCH AS WOULD HAVE MEDIATORS TO JESUS CHRIST: Alas! whosoever is so minded showeth plainly themselves to know nothing of Jesus Christ rightly. Is he who descended from heaven and vouchsafed to be conversant with sinners, commanding all sore vexed to seek to come unto him (who, hanging upon the cross, prayed first for his enemies) become now so untractable that he will not hear us without a person to be a mean?

O Lord! open the eyes of such, that they may clearly perceive thy infinite kindness, gentleness, and love toward mankind.

Above all precidentis[13] is to be observed, that what we ask of God ought to be profitable to ourselves and to others, and hurtful or dangerous to no man. Secondly, we must consider whether our petitions extendeth to spiritual or corporal things. Spiritual things, such as are deliverance from impiety, remission of sins, the gift of the Holy Ghost, and of life everlasting, should we desire absolutely, without any condition, by Jesus Christ, in whom alone all these are promised. And in asking hereof, we should not pray thus: O Father! forgive our sins if thou wilt. For his will he hath exprest, saying, "As I live, I desire not the death of a sinner, but rather that he convert, and live"; which immutable and solemn oath who calleth in doubt maketh God a liar, and so far as in him lieth would spoil God of his Godhead; for he can not be God except he be eternal and infallible verity. And John saith, "This is the testimony which God hath testified of his Son, that who (so) believeth in the Son hath eternal life" (1 John); to the verity whereof, we should stedfastly cleave; altho worldly dolor apprehend us. As David, ex-

[13] That is, above all these things.

iled from his kingdom and deprived of all
his glory, secluded not from God, but stedfastly believed reconciliation by the promise
made, notwithstanding that all creatures in
earth had refused, objected, and rebelled
against him: "Happy is the man whom thou
shall inspire, O Lord."

In asking corporal things, first let us inquire if we be at peace with God in our conscience by Jesus Christ, firmly believing our
sins to be remitted in his blood? Secondly,
let us inquire of our own hearts, if we know
temporal riches or substance not to come to
men by accident, fortune, or chance, neither
yet by the industry and diligence of man's
labor; but to be the liberal gift of God only
whereof we ought to laud and praise his goodness, wisdom, and providence alone?

WHAT SHOULD BE PRAYED FOR: And if
this we do truly acknowledge and confess, let
us boldly ask of him whatsoever is necessary
for us—as sustentation of this body; health
thereof; defense from misery; deliverance
from trouble; tranquility and peace to our
common weal; prosperous success in our vo-
cations, labors, and affairs, whatsoever they
be, which God will, we ask of all of him, to
certify us that all things stand in his regimen
and disposition. And also by asking and receiving these corporal commodities, we have

taste of his sweetness, and be inflamed with his love, that thereby our faith of reconciliation and remission of our sins may be exercised and take increase.

WHY GOD DIFFERETH OR PROLONGETH TO GRANT US OUR PETITIONS: But in asking for temporal things, we must observe, first, that if God differeth or prolongeth to grant our petitions, even so long that he seemeth apparently to reject us, yet let us not cease to call, prescribing him neither time, neither manner of deliverance; as it is written, "If he prolong time, abide patiently upon him," and also, "Let not the faithful be too hasty, for God sometime differeth, and will not hastily grant to the probation of our continuance," as the words of Jesus Christ testify; and also, that we may receive with greater gladness that which with ardent desire we long have looked for, as Anna, Sarah, and Elizabeth, after great ignominy of their barrenness and sterility, received fruit of their bosoms with joy. Secondly, because we know the Kirk[14] at all times to be under the cross, in asking temporal commodities, and special deliverance from trouble, let us offer unto God obedience, if it shall please his goodness we longer be exercised that we may patiently abide it; as David, desiring to be restored to

[14] Church.

his kingdom (what time he was exiled by his own son) offering to God obedience, saying, "If I have found favor in the presence of the Lord, he shall bring me home again; but if he shall say, Thou pleasest me not longer to bear authority, I am obedient: let him do what seemeth good unto him."

BETTER IT IS TO OBEY GOD THAN MAN: And the three children unto Nebuchadnezzar did say, "We know that our God whom we worship may deliver us; but if it shall not please him so to do, let it be known to thee, O king, that thy gods we will not worship" (Dan. 3). Here gave they a true confession of their perfect faith, knowing nothing to be impossible to the omnipotence of God; affirming also themselves to stand in his mercy; for otherwise the nature of man could not willingly give itself to so horrible a torment; but they offer unto God most humble obedience, to be delivered at his good pleasure and will. As we should do in all afflictions, for we know not what to ask or desire as we ought; that is, the frail flesh, opprest with fear and pain, desireth deliverance, ever abhorring and drawing back from obedience giving.

O Christian brethren, I write by experience; but the spirit of God calleth back the mind to obedience, that albeit (altho) it doth desire and abide for deliverance, yet

should it not repine against the good will of
God, but incessantly ask that it may abide
with patience; how hard this battle is no man
knoweth but he which in himself hath suffered trial.

THE PETITION OF THE SPIRIT: It is to be
noted that God sometime doth grant the petition of the spirit, while he yet differeth the
desire of the flesh. As who doubteth but God
did mitigate the heaviness of Joseph, altho
he sent not hasty deliverance in his long
imprisonment; and that as he gave him favor
in the sight of his jailor, so inwardly also
gave he unto him consolation in spirit. And
moreover God sometimes granteth the petition
of the spirit, where all utterly[15] he repelleth
the desire of the flesh; for the petition always
of the spirit is that we may attain to the
true felicity, whereunto we must needs enter
by tribulation and the final death, which both
the nature of man doth ever abhor, and therefore the flesh, under the cross and at the sight
of death, calleth and thirsts for hasty deliverance. But God, who alone knoweth what is expedient for us, sometime prolongeth the deliverance of his chosen, and sometime permit-
teth them to drink before the maturity of age
the bitter cup of corporal death, that thereby
they may receive medicine and cure from all

[15] Completely.

infirmity. For who doubteth that John the
Baptist desired to have seen more the days of
Jesus Christ, and to have been longer with
him in conversation? Or that Stephen would
not have labored more days in preaching
Christ's gospel, whom, nevertheless, he suffered hastily to taste of this general sentence?
And, albeit we see therefore no apparent help
to ourselves nor yet to others afflicted, let us
not cease to call, thinking our prayers to be
vain. For, whatsoever come of our bodies,
God shall give unspeakable comfort to the
spirit, and shall turn all to our commodities[16]
beyond our own expectation.

IMPEDIMENTS COMETH OF THE WEAKNESS
OF THE FLESH: The cause that I am so long
and tedious in this matter is for that (because) I know how hard the battle is betwixt
the spirit and the flesh under the heavy cross
of affliction, where no worldly defense but
present death does appear. I know the grudg-
ing and murmuring complaints of the flesh;
I know the anger, wrath, and indignation
which it conceiveth against God, calling all
his promises in doubt, and being ready every
hour utterly to fall from God. Against which
rests only faith, provoking us to call earnestly
and pray for assistance of God's spirit;
wherein if we continue, our most desperate

[16] Commodities, advantage or profit.

calamities shall he turn to gladness and to a prosperous end. To thee, O Lord, alone be praise, for with experience I write this and speak.

Where, for whom, and at what time we ought to pray, is not to be passed over with silence.

PRIVATE PRAYER: Private prayer, such as men secretly offer unto God by themselves, requires no special place; altho that Jesus Christ commandeth when we pray to enter into our chamber, and to close the door, and so to pray secretly unto our Father. Whereby he would that we should choose to our prayers such places as might offer least occasion to call us back from prayer; and also, that we should expel forth of our minds in time of our prayer all vain cogitations. For otherwise Jesus Christ himself doth observe no special place of prayer; for we find him sometime pray in Mount Olivet, sometime in the desert, sometime in the Temple, and in the garden. And Peter coveteth to pray upon the top of the house. Paul prayed in prison, and was heard of God. Who also commandeth men to pray in all places, lifting up unto God pure and clean hands; as we find that the prophets and most holy men did, whensoever danger or necessity required.

APPOINTED PLACES TO PRAY IN, MAY NOT

BE NEGLECTED: But public and common prayers should be used in place appointed for the assembly, from whence whosoever negligently extracted themselves is in no wise excusable. I mean not that to absent from that place is sin, because that place is more holy than another; for the whole earth created by God is equally holy. But the promise made that, "Wheresoever two or three be gathered together in my name, there shall I be in the midst of them," condemneth all such as contemneth the congregation gathered in his name. But mark well the word "gathered"; I mean not to hear piping, singing, or playing; nor to patter upon beads, or books whereof they have no understanding; nor to commit idolatry, honoring that for God which is no God in deed. For with such will I neither join myself in common prayer nor in receiving external sacraments; for in so doing I should affirm their superstitions and abominable idolatry, which I, by God's grace, never will do, neither counsel other to do, to the end.

WHAT IT IS TO BE GATHERED IN THE NAME OF CHRIST: This congregation which I mean, should be gathered in the name of Jesus Christ, that is, to laud and magnify God the Father for the infinite benefits they had received by his only Son our Lord. In this congregation should be distributed that mystical and last Supper of Jesus Christ without superstition, or any more ceremonies than he himself used and his apostles after him. And in distribution thereof, in this congregation should inquisition be made of the poor among them, and support provided till the time of their next convention, and it should be distributed amongst them. Also, in this congregation should be made common prayers, such as all men hearing might understand; that the hearts of all, subscrybing[17] to the voice of one, might with unfeigned and fervent mind say Amen. Whosoever doth withdraw himself from such a congregation (but alas, where shall it be found?) do declare themselves to be no members of Christ's body.

FOR WHOM, AND AT WHAT TIME WE SHOULD PRAY: Now there remaineth, for whom, and at what time, we should pray. For all men, and at all times, doth Paul command that we should pray. And principally for such of the household of faith as suffer persecution; and for commonwealths tyrannously opprest incessantly should we call, that God of his mercy and power will withstand the violence of such tyrants.

GOD'S SENTENCE MAY BE CHANGED: And when we see the plagues of God, as hunger,

[17] Subscribing, agreeing.

pestilence, or weir[18] coming or appearing to ring[19] then should we, with lamentable voices and repenting hearts, call unto God, that it would please his infinite mercy to withdraw his hand; which thing, if we do unfeignedly, he will without doubt revoke his wrath, and in the midst of his fury think upon mercy; as we are taught in the Scripture by his infallible and eternal verities. As in Exodus God saith, "I shall destroy this nation from the face of the earth"; and when Moses addrest himself to pray for them, the Lord proceedeth, saying, "Suffer me that I may utterly destroy them." And then Moses falleth down upon his face, and forty days continueth in prayer for the safety of the people; for whom at the last he obtained forgiveness. David, in the vehement plague, lamentably called unto God. And the king of Nineveh said, "Who can tell? God may turn and repent, and cease from his fierce wrath, that we perish not." Which examples and scriptures are not written in vain, but to certify us that God of his own native goodness will mitigate his plagues (by our prayers offered by Jesus Christ), altho he hath threatened to punish or presently doth punish. Which he doth testify by his own words, saying, "If I have prophesied against any nation or people, that they

18 War.   19 To reign, to prevail.

shall be destroyed, if they repent of their
iniquity, it shall repent me of the evil which
I have spoken against them'' (Jer. 18). This
I write, lamenting the great coldness of men,
which under so long scourges of God is nothing kindled to pray by repentance, but care-
lessly sleepeth in a wicked life; even as tho
the continual wars, urgent famine, and quoti-
dian plagues of pestilence, and other conta-
gious, insolent,[20] and strange maladies were
not the present signs of God's wrath, provoked by our iniquities.

A PLAGUE THREATENED TO ENGLAND: O
England! let thy intestine battle, and do-
mestical murder provoke thee to purity of
life, according to the word which openly hath
been proclaimed in thee, otherwise the cup
of the Lord's wrath thou shalt drink! The
multitude shall not escape, but shall drink
the dregs and have the cup broken upon their
heads. For judgment beginneth in the house
of the Lord, and commonly the least offender
is first punished, to provoke the more wicked
to repentance. But, O Lord! infinite in
mercy, if thou shalt punish, make not consum-
mation, but cut away the proud and luxuriant
branches which bear no fruit: and preserve
the commonwealths of such as give succor
and harbor to thy contemned messengers,

[20] Insolent, unaccustomed.

which long have suffered exile in desert. And let thy kingdom shortly come that sin may be ended, death devoured, thy enemies confounded; that we thy people, by thy majesty delivered, may obtain everlasting joy and felicity, through Jesus Christ our Savior, to whom be all honor and praise for ever. AMEN.

Hasten, Lord, and tarry not.

A Prayer From the Syrian Clementine Liturgy

O God, who art the unsearchable abyss of peace, the ineffable sea of love, the fountain of blessings and the bestower of affection, who sendest peace to those that receive it; open to us this day the sea of thy love, and water us with plenteous streams from the riches of thy grace. Make us children of quietness and heirs of peace. Enkindle in us the fire of thy love; strengthen our weakness by thy power; bind us closely to thee and to each other in one firm and indissoluble bond of unity. AMEN.

Meditation of the Soul on Its God

Written in 1579

BY

SAINT THERESA OF JESUS

SAINT THERESA

Spanish mystic and monastic reformer; born at Avila, Old Castile, March 28, 1515; died at Alva, October 4, 1582. In her eighteenth year she left her parental home secretly and entered the Carmelite Monastery of the Incarnation at Avila. She suffered much from illness and during this time experienced periods of spiritual ecstasy. Her religious exercises reached an unusual degree of asceticism leading to self-inflicted tortures and mortifications. On St. Peter's Day of 1559 she became convinced of Christ's actual bodily presence with her. During the last three years of her life Theresa founded convents at Villanueva de la Xara in northern Andulusia (1580), Palencia (1580), Soria (1581), Burgos, and at Granada (1582). Seventeen nunneries, all but one founded by her, and as many men's cloisters felt her reform activity, lasting twenty years. Forty years after her death she was canonized, and her church reveres her as the "seraphic virgin." Her best-known treatises are: "The Life of S. Teresa of Jesus" (English translation, London, 1888), "The Way of Perfection" (English translation, 1852), and "The Interior Castle" (English translation, 1852).

Meditations

1. O my God, infinite Wisdom, without measure and without bounds, above all understanding either by angels or by men; love, who dost love me more than I can love myself or than I can conceive; why do I wish for more than thou dost will to give me? Why do I weary myself in praying for my needs, since thou already knowest all my thoughts could imagine or my heart could wish for, while I am ignorant of what will profit or injure me.

2. Perhaps what my soul fancies would be its gain might be its ruin. If I ask thee to free me from a cross by which thou seekest to mortify me, what do I ask thee, O my God?

3. If I entreat thee to send me such a trial, perhaps it may be beyond my patience, which is too weak to bear this heavy burden; or if I were to endure it, but were wanting in humility, I might fancy I had performed some great deed, while thou, O my God, didst do it all. When I seek for greater sufferings, I do not wish for what might injure my good

name, lest it might prevent my serving thee, altho I care nothing for honor for my own sake; yet perhaps the very means I think would hinder me might further my one desire of laboring for thee. I could say more, O Lord, to show how little I know myself, but as thou surely knowest this, why should I speak of it?

4. I write this, so that when misery again overwhelms me, and reason is blinded, I may read it and may find my better self again. Often, O my God, when I feel most wretched, most weak, most cowardly, do I try to recall my former self, who called herself thy servant and thought the grace she had received from thee would suffice to arm her against all the struggles of life.

5. Ah no, my God! Let me no longer trust my own judgment as to what to ask of thee; dispose of me as thou pleasest. This do I ask, which alone can bring me happiness, for I should bring about my own ruin, if thou, O my God, wert to satisfy all my cravings. How vain is man's wisdom, and how dangerous are his plans! May thy providence supply my need. O let my soul serve thee according to thy will, and not my own.

6. Punish me not by granting prayers or wishes at variance with thy love, which I desire may dwell within me. Make me die to

self; let another, greater and better than I am, live within me, that I may serve him; let him live and give me life (Gal. 2:20); let him reign that I may be his slave—I seek no other liberty, for none can be free while separated from the Most High. What more abject or more miserable serf than the soul which has broken loose from the hands of its Creator?

7. Happy the souls imprisoned by the fetters and chains of God's gifts and mercy, and too strongly bound and helpless to free themselves. "Love is strong as death and hard as hell" (Song of Songs 8:6).

8. Oh, that we were but slain by this love, and locked in this divine dungeon, from whence, ah, from whence there is no escape, or rather no fear of being cast forth. But wo is me, O Lord! during this mortal life we live in constant danger of losing the life that is eternal.

9. O life, enemy of my joy, why is it not lawful to put an end to thee? I endure thee, for God is pleased to prolong thee; I sustain thee for thou art his; do not betray me nor harm me in return. And yet, ah Lord, "Woe is me that my sojourning is prolonged" (Ps. 119:5). Time is short wherewith to purchase eternity, yet how long a day or even an hour appears, laden with the risk and the dread of offending thee.

10. Free-will, thou art the slave of thy liberty, unless established in the fear and love of thy Creator! When will that blessed day arrive in which, absorbed in the infinite ocean of supreme truth, thou wilt no longer possess the power nor the wish to sin, for thou wilt be freed from all misery, and united with the life of thy God!

11. God is happy, for he rejoices in, he knows, and loves himself, without the possibility of doing otherwise. He is not, nor can he be, at liberty to forget or to cease to love himself, nor would such power be a perfection in him. Thou wilt enter into thy rest O my soul, when thou art united with this Sovereign Good, when thou knowest what he knows and lovest what he loves, and dost rejoice in what rejoices him.

12. Then wilt thou lose the fickleness of thy will; then, ah then, thou wilt change no more, for the grace of God, which can do all things, will render thee so perfect a partaker of his divine nature (2 Pet. 1:4) that thou wilt no longer have the power or the wish to forget the Supreme Good, nor to cease to enjoy thy union with his love. Blessed are those whose names are written in the book of life (Luke 10:20). But, O my soul, if thou art among their number, "Why art thou sad, and why dost thou trouble me?" (Ps. 41:6).

13. "Hope in the Lord, because I will yet confess to him" (Ps. 41: 12) my sins and his mercies: of which I will make a song of praise: this will I mingle with incessant sighs after him, my Savior and my God. It may be that a day will come when "my glory shall sing to him" (Ps. 29: 13) and my conscience be no more troubled; when weeping and tears shall be no more. Meanwhile "in hope and silence shall my strength be" (Isa. 30: 15). Rather would I live and die in the hope of eternal life than possess all created beings and riches as my own, for they must all pass away. Forsake me not, O Lord, for "in Thee do I trust, let not my hope be confounded" (Ps. 30). Make me serve thee faithfully, and in all else, do with me what thou wilt.

A Prayer From the Sarum Breviary

We beseech thee, O Lord, let our hearts be graciously enlightened by thy holy radiance, that we may serve thee without fear in holiness and righteousness all the days of our life; that so we may escape the darkness of this world, and by thy guidance attain the land of eternal brightness; through thy mercy, O blessed Lord, who dost live and govern all things, world without end. AMEN.

A Prayer of Charles Jean Besson

O Lord, I fling myself with all my weakness and misery into thy ever-open arms. I know that I am ignorant and much mistaken about myself. Thou who seest in very truth, look mercifully on me. Lay thy healing hand upon my wounds. Pour the life-giving balm of thy love into my heart. Do for me what I have not the courage to do for myself. Save me in spite of myself. May I be thine—wholly thine, and at all costs thine. In humiliation, in poverty, in suffering, in self-abnegation, thine. Thine in the way thou knowest to be most fitting, in order that thou mightest be now and ever mine. Thou art my Strength and my Redeemer. I am thy poor little creature, dependent on thy merciful charity alone. AMEN.

Rules and Instructions for a Holy Life

BY

ROBERT LEIGHTON

ARCHBISHOP OF GLASGOW

ROBERT LEIGHTON

Author of the well-known "Rules and Instructions for a Holy Life," and characterized "as perhaps the rarest flower that has grown out of Scotch theology," was the second son of Dr. Alexander Leighton. He was born (probably in London) 1611; died in London, June 25, 1684. In 1641 he was licensed by the presbytery of Edinburgh, and in that same year was ordained and inducted into the parish of Newbattle. In 1652 he was appointed principal of the University of Edinburgh. Here he remained nine years, and Bishop Burnet testifies to his remarkable influence over the students. Leighton's "Praelectiones Theologicæ" are extant to show the kind of Latin orations which he delivered weekly. Most of the "Sermons" and the "Commentary on the First Epistle of Peter" were the work of the Newbattle period. The Restoration placed on the throne an absolute king with a rooted determination to force episcopacy on Scotland. Leighton, after much reluctance, was forced by the king himself to become one of the bishops of the new ecclesiastical *régime*, but with characteristic modesty chose for himself Dunblame, the poorest of the new dioceses, from which in 1669 he was transferred to the archdiocese of Glasgow. He resigned in 1674.

Leighton published nothing during his lifetime, and requested that his papers should be destroyed. His writings were first edited by his friend Dr. James Fall. The principal are: "Sermons" (London, 1692); "A Practical Commentary upon the... First Epistle General of St. Peter" (part i, York, 1693; part ii, London, 1694); "Praelectiones Theologicæ" (London, 1693); and "Three Posthumous Tracts" (1708), including the well-known "Rules and Instructions for a Holy Life" (new ed., Oxford, 1905).

Rules and Instructions for a Holy Life

For disposing you the better to observe these rules, and profit by them, be pleased to take the following advice.

1. Put all your trust in the special and singular mercy of God, that he for his mercy's sake, and of his mere goodness, will help and bring you to perfection; not that absolute perfection is attainable here, but the meaning is, to high degrees of that spiritual and divine life, which is always growing, and tending toward the absolute perfection above; and which in some persons comes nearer to that, and riseth higher even here, than in the most. If with hearty and fervent desires, you do continually wish and long for it; and, with most humble devotion, daily pray unto God, and call for it, and with all diligence do busily labor to come to it, undoubtedly it will be given you; for you must not think it sufficient to use exercises, as tho they had such virtues in them, that of themselves alone, they could make such as use them, perfect; for neither those, nor any other, whatever they be, can of themselves, by their use only, bring unto perfection. But our merciful Lord God,

of his own goodness, when you seek with hearty desires and fervent sighings, maketh you to find it: when you ask daily with devout prayer, then he giveth it to you; and when you continually with unwearied labor, knock perseveringly, then he doth mercifully open unto you; and because those exercises do teach you to seek, ask, and knock; yea, they are no other than very devout petitions, seekings, and spiritual pulsations for the merciful help of God; therefore they are very profitable means of coming to perfection by God's grace.

2. Let no particular exercise hinder your public and standing duties to God and your neighbors; but for these rather intermit the other for a time, and then return to them as soon as you can.

3. If, in time of your spiritual exercise, you find yourself drawn to any better, or to as good a contemplation, as that is; follow the tract of that good motion so long as it shall last.

4. Always take care to follow such exercises of devout thoughts with putting in practise such lessons as they contain and excite.

5. Tho at first you feel no sweetness in such exercises; yet be not discouraged, nor induced to leave them; but continue in them faithfully, whatsoever pain or s p i r i t u a l trouble you feel in doing them for God and

his honor; and, finding no other present fruit, yet you shall have an excellent reward for your diligent labor and your pure intentions; and let not your falling short of these rules, nor your daily manifold imperfections and faults, dishearten you; but continue stedfast in your desires, purposes, and endeavors; and ever ask the best, aim at the best, and hope the best, being sorry that you can do no better; and they shall be a most acceptable sacrifice in the sight of God, "and in due time you shall reap, if you faint not"; and of all such instructions let your rule be to follow them as much as you can; but not too scrupulously thinking your labor lost if you do not exactly answer them in every thing; purpose still better, and by God's grace all shall be well.

I

Rule 1. Exercise thyself in the knowledge and deep consideration of our Lord God, calling humbly to mind how excellent and incomprehensible he is; and this knowledge shalt thou rather endeavor to obtain by fervent desire and devout prayer, than by high study and outward labor; it is the singular gift of God, and certainly very precious. Pray then, 2. "Most gracious Lord, whom to know is the very bliss and felicity of man's soul; and yet no one can know thee unless thou wilt open and show thyself unto him; vouchsafe of thy infinite mercy now and ever to enlighten my mind to know thee and thy most holy and perfect will, to the honor and glory of thy name. AMEN.''

3. Then lift up thy heart to consider (not with too great violence, but soberly) the eternal and infinite power of God, who created all things by his excellent wisdom; his unmeasurable goodness, and incomprehensible love; for he is very and only God, most excellent, most high, most glorious, the everlasting and unchangeable goodness, an eternal substance, a charity infinite, so excellent and ineffable in himself, that all dignity, perfection, and goodness, that is possible to be spoken or thought of, can not sufficiently express the smallest part thereof.

4. Consider that he is the natural place, the center, and rest of thy soul; if thou then think of the most blessed Trinity, muse not too much thereon; but, with devout and obedient faith, meekly and lowly adore and worship.

5. Consider Jesus, the Redeemer and Husband of thy soul, and walk with him as becomes a chaste spouse, with reverence and lowly shamefulness, obedience, and submission.

Robert Leighton

6. Then turn to the deep, profound consideration of thyself, thine own nothingness, and thy extreme defilement and pollution, thy natural aversion from God, and that thou must by conversion to him again, and union with him, be made happy.

7. Consider thyself and all creatures, as nothing, in comparison of thy Lord! that so thou mayest not only be content, but desirous to be unknown; or, being known, to be contemned and despised of all men, yet without thy fault or deserving as much, as thou canst.

8. "O God, infuse into my heart thy heavenly light and blessed love, that I may know and love thee above all things; and above all things loath and abhor myself. Grant that I may be so ravished in the wonder and love of thee that I may forget myself and all things; feel neither prosperity nor adversity; may not fear to suffer all the pains of this world rather, than to be parted and drawn away from thee, whose perfections infinitely exceed all thought and understanding. O, let me find thee more inwardly and verily present with me than I am with myself; and make me most circumspect how I do conduct myself in the presence of thee, my holy Lord.

"Cause me always to remember how everlasting and constant is the love, thou bearest toward me; such a love and continual care, as tho thou hadst no other creatures in heaven or earth beside me.''

9. Then aspire to great contrition for thy sins, and hatred of them; and, abhorring thyself for them, then crave pardon through the blood of Jesus Christ; and then offer up thyself, soul and body, and oblation or sacrifice in and through him; as they did of old, laying wood on the altar, and then burning up all; so this shall be a sacrifice of sweet savor, and very acceptable to God.

10. Offer all that thou hast, to be nothing, to use nothing of all that thou hast about thee and is called thine but to his honor and glory; and resolve through his grace, to use all the powers of thy soul, and every member of thy body, to his service, as formerly thou hast done to sin.

11. Consider the passion of thy Lord, how he was buffeted, scourged, reviled, stretched with nails on the cross, and hung on it three long hours; suffered all the contempt and shame, and all the inconceivable pain of it, for thy sake.

12. Then turn thy heart to him, humbly saying, ''Lord Jesus, whereas I daily fall, and am ready to sin, vouchsafe me grace to rise again; let me never presume, but always most meekly and humbly acknowledge my wretchedness and frailty, and repent, with a firm pur-

pose to amend; and let me not despair because of my great frailty; but ever trust in thy most loving mercy, and readiness to forgive.''

II

1. Thou wilt have much to do in mortifying thy five senses, which must all be shut up in the crucified humility of Jesus Christ, and be as if they were plainly dead.

2. Thou must now learn to have a continual eye inwardly to thy soul and spiritual life, as thou hast used heretofore to have all thy mind and regard to outward pleasure and worldly things.

3. Thou must submit and give thyself up to the discipline of Jesus, and become his scholar, resigning and compelling thyself to obey him in all things; so that thou do utterly and perfectly cast away thy own will from thee, and do nothing without his license. At every word thou shalt speak, at every morsel thou shalt eat, at every motion of every joint or member of thy body, thou must ask leave of him in thy heart; and ask thyself, whether, having so done, that be according to his will and holy example, and with sincere intention of his glory. Hence,

4. Even the most necessary actions of thy life, tho lawful, yet must thus be offered

up with true intention unto God, in union with the blessed merits of Christ, saying, "Lord Jesus, bind up in the merits of thy blessed senses all my powers and senses, that I never hereafter use them to any sensuality."

5. Thus labor to come to this union of thy senses in God and thy Lord Jesus, and remain so fast to the cross that thou never part from it; and still thy body and all thy senses employ as in the presence of thy Lord God; and commit all things to the most trusty providence of thy loving Lord, who will then order all things delightfully for thee; reckon all things beside, as naught; and thus mayest thou come to wonderful illuminations and spiritual influence from the Lord thy God.

6. If, for his love, thou wouldst perfectly renounce, and forsake all things; thou must so crucify thyself and so love and desire God, that in this most stedfast union to the will of God, thou mayest be ready to offer thyself, to suffer for his honor and this purely for his will and pleasure.

7. Thou must keep thy memory pure from all strange thoughts, fancies, and imaginations; and it must be adorned with holy meditation and virtues of Christ's holy crucified life and passion; that God may continually rest therein.

Prayer

8. "Lord, instead of knowing thee, I have sought to know wickedness and sin; and, whereas my will and desire were created to love thee, I have lost that love, and declined to the creatures; while my memory ought to be filled with thee, I have painted it with the imagery of innumerable fancies, not only of all creatures, but of all sinful wickedness. Oh, blot out these by thy blood, and imprint thine own image in my soul, blessed Jesus, by that blood that issued from thy most loving heart when thou hangedst on the cross; so unite my will to thy most holy will that I may have no will but thine, and may be most heartily and fully content with whatsoever thou shalt do to me in this world; yea, if thou shouldst so that I sin not against thee, but retain thy love, make me suffer the greatest pains."

III

Rule 1. Exercise thyself to a perfect renunciation of all things which may impede this union; mortifying in thee every thing that is not God, nor for God, or which he willeth and loveth not; resigning and yielding up to the high pleasure of God all love and affection for transitory things; desire neither to have nor to hold them, nor bestow or give them, but only for the pure love and honor of God; put away superfluous things, and affect not even things necessary.

2. Mortify all affection to and seeking of thyself, which is so natural to men, in all the good they desire, in all the good they do, and in all the evil they suffer; yea, by the inordinate love of the gifts and graces of God, instead of himself, they fall into spiritual pride, gluttony, and greediness.

3. Mortify all affection to and delight in meat and drink, and vain thoughts and fancies, which, tho they proceed not to consent, yet defile the soul, and grieve the Holy Ghost, and do great damage to the spiritual life.

4. Imprint on thy heart the image of Jesus crucified; the impressions of his humility, poverty, mildness, and all his holy virtues; let thy thoughts of him turn into affection, and thy knowledge into love; for the love of God doth most purely work in the mortification of nature; the life of the spirit, purifying the higher powers of the soul, begets a departure from all creatures, and flowing into God.

5. Solitude, silence, and a strict keeping of the heart, are the foundation of a spiritual life.

6. Do all thy necessary outward works

without anxiety, and keep thy mind always elevated to God, following more the inward exercise of love, than the outward acts of virtue.

7. To this can no man come, unless he be delivered from all things below God, and be so swallowed up in God, as to contemn and despise himself and all things; for the pure love of God maketh the spirit pure and simple, and so free that without pain or labor it can at all times turn and recollect itself in God.

8. Mortify all bitterness of heart toward thy neighbor, and all complacency in thyself, all vainglory and desire of esteem, in words and deeds, in gifts and graces. To this thou wilt come by a more perfect knowledge of thy own vileness, and by knowing God to be the fountain of all grace and goodness.

9. Mortify all affection to inward, sensible, spiritual delight in grace, and to the following devotion with sensible sweetness in the lower faculties of the soul, which in themselves are not real sanctity and holiness, but certain gifts of God to help our infirmity.

10. Mortify all curious search, speculation, and knowledge of unnecessary things, human or divine; for the perfect life of a Christian consisteth not in high knowledge, but in profound meekness; in holy simplicity, and in ardent love of God; wherein we ought to

crucify all affection to ourselves, and all things below God; yea, to sustain pain and dereliction, that we may be perfectly united to God, and perfectly swallowed up in him.

11. Mortify all undue scruples of mind and trust in the goodness of God; for our doubts and scruples often arise from inordinate self love, and therefore vex us; they do no good, nor do they work any real amendment in us; they cloud the soul, darken faith and cool love; and it is only the stronger beams of these that can dispel them; and the stronger this faith is in us, and the warmer divine love is, so much the more is the soul excited and enabled to all the parts of holiness, to mortification of passions and lusts, to mere patience in adversity, and to more thankfulness in all states.

12. Mortify all impatience under pain and trouble, whether from the hand of God or man, all desire of revenge, all resentment of injuries; and by the pure love of God, love thy persecutors, as if they were thy dearest friends.

13. Finally, mortify thy own will in all things, with full resignation of thyself to suffer all dereliction outward and inward, all pain, and pressures, and desolations, and this for the pure love of God; for from self-love and self-will spring all sin and all pain.

Prayer

14. "O Jesus, my Savior, thy blessed humility! I impress it on my heart; make me sensible of thy infinite dignity, and of my own vileness, that I may hate myself, as a thing of naught, and be willing to be despised, and trodden upon by all, that I may still retain these words, I am nothing, I have nothing, I can do nothing, and I desire nothing, but one."

IV

1. Never do any thing with singular affection, being too earnest, or too much given to it; but, with continual meekness of heart and mind, lie at the foot of God, and say, "Lord, I desire nothing, either in myself, or in any creature, save only to know and execute thy blessed will; saying always in thy heart, Lord, what wouldst thou have me to do? transform my will into thine, swallow up my affections with thy love, and with an insatiable desire to honor thee and despise myself."

2. If thou aspire to attain perfect union with God, know that it requireth utter renunciation of all sin, yea, of all creatures, and of thyself particularly; even that thy mind and understanding, thy affections and desires, thy memory and fancy, be made bare of all

things in the world, and of all sensual pleasure in them, so that thou wouldst be content if the bread which thou eatest had no more savor than a stone; and yet, for his honor who created bread, thou art pleased that it savoreth well; but yet, from the pleasure thou hast in it, turn thy heart to his praise and love, who made it.

3. The more perfectly thou livest in abstraction of mind from all creatures, the more purely shalt thou have the fruition of the Lord thy God, and shalt live a more heavenly and angelic life. Therefore,

4. Labor above all things most exactly to forsake all for him, and chiefly to forsake and contemn thyself, loving him purely, and in a manner forgetting thyself and all things, for the vehement love of him; thus thy mind will run so much upon him that thou wilt take no heed what is sweet or bitter; nor wilt thou consider time or place, nor mark one person from another, for the wonder and love of thy Lord, God, and the desire of his blessed will, pleasure, and honor in all things; and, whatsoever good thou dost, know and think that God doth it, and not thou.

5. Choose always, to the best of thy skill, what is most for God's honor, most like unto Christ and his example, most profitable to thy neighbor, most against thy own will, and

least serviceable to thy own praise and exaltation.

6. If thou continue faithful in this spiritual work, God at length will hear thy knocking, and will deliver thee from all thy spiritual trouble, from all the tumult of fancies, and from all earthly affections, which thou canst by no better means put away, than by continual and fervent desire of the love of God.

7. Do not at any time hinder his working by following thine own will; for, behold, how much thou dost the more perfectly forsake thine own will, and love of thyself, and of all worldly things, so much the more closely shalt thou be united to God, and increase in his true and pure love.

V

1. If thou still above all things seek this union, thou must pour thy whole will into the high pleasure of God; and, whatsoever befalls thee, thou must be without murmuring of heart, accepting it most joyfully for his love, whose will and work it is.

2. Let thy great joy and comfort ever more be, to have his pleasure done in thee, tho in pains, sickness, persecutions, oppressions, or inward griefs and pressures of heart, coldness or barrenness of mind, darkening of thy un-

derstanding and senses, or any temptations spiritual or bodily. And

3. Under any of these, be always wary thou turn not to sinful delights, nor to sensual and carnal pleasures, nor set thy heart on vain things, seeking comfort thereby, nor in any wise be idle, but always, as thou canst, compel thyself to some good spiritual exercise or bodily work; and, tho they then be unsavory to thee, yet are they not the less, but the more, acceptable to God.

4. Take all afflictions, as tokens of God's love to thee, and trials of thy love to him, and purposes of kindness to enrich thee, and increase more plentifully in thee his blessed gifts and spiritual graces, if thou persevere faithfully to the end; not leaving off the vehement desire of his love and of thy own perfection.

5. Offer up thyself wholly to him, and fix the point of thy love upon his most blessed increated love, and there let thy heart rest and delight, and be, as it were, resolved and melted most happily into the blessed Godhead; and then take this as a token, and be assured by it, that God will grant thy holy desire; then shalt thou feel, in a manner, no difference between honor and shame, joy and sorrow; but, whatsoever thou perceivest to appertain to the honor of thy Lord, be it ever

so hard and unpleasant to thyself, thou wilt
heartily embrace it, yea, with all thy might
follow and desire it; yet, when thou hast done
what is possible for thee, thou wilt think thou
hast done nothing at all, yea, thou wilt be
ashamed, and detest thyself, that thou hast
so wretchedly and imperfectly served so noble
and worthy a Lord; and therefore thou wilt
desire and endeavor every hour to do greater
and more perfect things than hitherto thou
hast done, forgetting the things, that are behind, and pressing forward, etc.

6. If thou hast in any measure attained to
love and abide in God, then mayest thou keep
the powers of thy soul and thy senses, as it
were, shut up in God, from gadding out to any
worldly thing or vanity, as much as possible,
where they have so joyful a security; satiate
thy soul in him, and in all other things still
see his blessed presence.

7. Whatsoever befalleth thee, receive it not
from the hand of any creature, but from him
alone, and render back all to him, seeking in
all things his pleasure and honor, the purifying and subduing of thyself. What can harm
thee, when all must first touch God, within
whom thou hast enclosed thyself?

8. When thou perceivest thyself thus
united to God, and thy soul more nearly
joined to him than to thine own body, then

shalt thou know his everlasting, incomprehensible, and ineffable goodness, and the true nobleness of thy soul, that came from him and was made to be reunited to him.

9. If thou wouldst ascend to thy Lord God, thou must climb up by the wounds of his blessed humanity, that remain, as it were, for that use; and, when thou art got up there, thou wouldst rather suffer death than willingly commit any sin.

10. Entering into Jesus, thou casteth thyself into an infinite sea of goodness, that more easily drowns and happily swallows thee up than the ocean does a drop of water. Then shalt thou be hidden and transformed in him, and shalt often be, as thinking without thought, and knowing without knowledge, and loving without love, comprehended by him whom thou canst not comprehend.

VI

1. Too much desire to please men greatly obstructs the pleasing of God.

2. Too great earnestness and delight in bodily work and external actions destroy the tranquility and calmness of the mind.

3. Cast all thy care on God, and commit all to his good pleasure; praise and applaud him in all things, small and great; forsake

thy own will, and deliver up thyself freely and cheerfully to the will of God, without reserve or exception, in prosperity and adversity, to have or to want, to live or to die.

4. Disunite thy heart from all things, and unite it only to God.

5. Remember often and devoutly the life and passion, the death and resurrection, of our Savior Jesus.

6. Descant not on other men's deeds, but consider thine own; forget other men's faults, and remember thine own.

7. Never think highly of thyself, nor despise any other man.

8. Keep silence and retirement as much as thou canst; and through God's grace they will keep thee from snares and offenses.

9. Lift up thy heart often to God, and desire in all things his assistance.

10. Let thy heart be filled and wholly taken up with the love of God, and of thy neighbor; do all that thou dost in sincere charity and love.

The sum is: (1) Remember always the presence of God. (2) Rejoice always in the will of God. And (3) direct all to the glory of God.

VII

1. Little love, little trust: but great love brings great confidence.

2. That is a blessed hope, that doth not slacken us in our duty nor make us secure, but both increaseth a cheerful will and gives greater strength to mortification and all obedience.

3. What needst thou, or why laborest thou about so many things; think upon one, desire and love one, and thou shalt find great rest. Therefore,

4. Wherever thou be, let this voice of God be still in thine ear; my son, return inwardly to thy heart, abstract thyself from all things, and mind me only. Thus,

5. With a pure mind in God, divested of the memory of all things, remaining immoveably in him, thou shalt desire nothing, but him alone; as tho there were nothing else in the world except him and thee only; that all thy faculties and powers, being thus recollected unto God, thou mayest become one spirit with him.

6. Fix thy mind on thy crucified Savior, and remember continually his great meekness, love, and obedience, his perfect chastity, his unspeakable patience, and all the holy virtues of his humanity.

7. Think on his mighty power and infinite goodness; how he created and redeemed thee, how he justifieth thee, and worketh in thee all virtues, graces, and goodness; and thus remember him, until thy memory turn into love and affection. Therefore,

8. Draw thy mind thus from all creatures unto a certain silence, and rest from the jangling and company of all things below God; and, when thou canst come to this, then is thy heart a place meet and ready for thy Lord God to abide in, there to talk with thy soul.

9. True humility gaineth God Almighty, and maketh thee meet to receive all graces and gifts; but, alas, who can say that he hath this blessed meekness, it being so hard, so uncertain, so secret and unknown a thing, to forsake and mortify perfectly and exactly thyself, and that most venomous worm of all goodness, vainglory?

10. Commit all to the high providence of God, and suffer nothing to enter into thy heart, save only God; all things on the earth are too base to take up thy love or care, or to trouble thy noble heart, thy immortal and heavenly mind; let them care and sorrow, or rejoice about these things, who are of the world, for whom Christ would not pray.

11. Thou canst not please, nor serve two

masters at once; thou canst not love divers and contrary things; if then thou wouldst know what thou lovest, mark well what thou thinkest most upon; leave earth, and have heaven; leave the world, and have God.

12. All sin and vice spring from our own will; all virtue and perfection come and grow from the mortifying of it, and the resigning of it wholly to the pleasure and will of God.

A Prayer of Joachim Embden

Grant us grace to rest from all sinful deeds and thoughts, to surrender ourselves wholly unto thee, and to keep our souls still before thee like a still lake; that so the beams of thy grace may be mirrored therein, and may kindle in our hearts the glow of faith and love and prayer. May we, through such stillness and hope, find strength and gladness in thee, O God, now and forevermore. AMEN.

WITHDRAWN FROM
OHIO NORTHERN
UNIVERSITY LIBRARY

GAYLORD   PRINTED IN U.S.A.